The Japanese Education System

System

by

Yasuhiro Nemoto

Universal Publishers/uPUBLISH.com

Parkland, Florida USA

1999

Published by

Universal Publishers/uPUBLISH.com

Parkland, Florida USA

1999

ISBN: 1-58112-799-5

http://www.upublish.com/books/nemoto.htm

Table of Contents

Chapter 1: Introduction

The Japanese education system is admired by many foreign educators, who note that Japanese students do better than their American counterparts in international math and science tests. Disciplined Japanese students obey teachers, rarely commit school violence and have little contact with drugs or alcohol. Some American education analysts insist that the adoption of the Japanese system by the United States would provide American children with a good educational foundation, and reduce school problems such as drug abuse, violence and truancy.

Because of the strong link between education and national development, Japan's post-World War II economic miracle is often attributed to its school system. It is therefore only natural that foreign educators should be interested in Japanese school education. Japan, an economic powerhouse second only to the United States, rose from the ashes of catastrophe at the end of the war by means of government-led economic policies. Realizing that national prosperity depended on school outcomes, the Japanese government extended its influence in education by centralizing the school system and standardizing the school curriculum. Under this national policy, children were disciplined and educated to become obedient, hardworking workers, who would contribute specifically to catching up with or surpassing western technologies.

Structure of the School System

The Japanese school system has a 6-3-3-4 system: six years of elementary school, three years each for middle school (lower-secondary school) and high school (upper-secondary school) and four years for university. There are also kindergarten and nursery schools for pre-school children.

Japanese law requires all children between the ages of six and 15 to receive education, either in an elementary school and a middle school or in a special school for the blind, the deaf or the otherwise handicapped. All children receive a general education appropriate to their level of physical and mental development. High schools, which provide both general and specialized education, are not compulsory; but admission to higher educational institutions is limited to students who have completed high school education. Colleges of technology admit middle school graduates and require five years of study (five and a half years for the merchant marine course); graduates are awarded the title of associate.

History

The modern education system in Japan began with the Education Order of 1872. The Education Ministry, established in 1871, issued in 1886 the Elementary School Order, the Middle School Order, the Imperial University Order and the Normal School Order, which established a comprehensive school system. The ministry determined the national curriculum and compiled and authorized textbooks for elementary and middle schools. Local school officials had to comply with all of the ministry's education policies.

After World War II, the United States occupied Japan and made liberal proposals for reform of the Japanese school system. In 1947, the Fundamental Law of Education and the School Education Law were enacted and a 6-3-3-4 system was set up on the principle of equal educational opportunity.   High schools were introduced in 1948, offering full-time and part-time courses; a correspondence course was added in 1961.   In 1949 universities began under a new system, and a provisional system of junior colleges was introduced in 1950. The permanent system for junior colleges was established in 1964 through an amendment to the School Education Law.

Common Education

"All people shall have the right to receive an equal education correspondent to their ability, as provided for by law. All people shall be obligated to have all boys and girls under their protection receive ordinary education as provided for by law. Such compulsory education shall be free." (Constitution of Japan, Article 26)

Parents are obliged to have their children receive common education in elementary and middle schools: home schooling, which exists in the United States, is prohibited in Japan. Public elementary and middle school tuition is funded by the government, so that all children receive an adequate education, regardless of family income. However public high schools do charge for tuition; and students in private elementary, middle and high schools pay much higher tuition fees.

Central government supplies textbooks free of charge to all children enrolled in public and private elementary schools and middle schools. This system was introduced in fiscal 1963, to put into practice the spirit of the Constitution. In fiscal 1994, ¥43.4 billion (U.S.$347.2 million, based on an exchange rate of ¥125 to the dollar) was spent on a total of 136.15 million textbooks for about

12.98 million schoolchildren. Students pay for their own notebooks, pens and other necessary school supplies.

The State Curriculum

The Education Ministry sets the national curricula for all public schools, from kindergarten to high school, to ensure standardized education. Under this system, each school creates its own curriculum conforming to the provisions of the School Education Law, the Enforcement Regulations of this law, and the Course of Study, while taking into account its own circumstances and the situation of the community.

The ministry's "Enforcement Regulations for the School Education Law" determine the minimum number of weeks of school per year and the subjects to be offered. The Course of Study (*Gakushu Shidoyoryo*) presents guidelines for the objectives and standard content of each school subject; it specifies the names of elective subjects, and regulates the content of the curriculum in detail. The Course of Study has recently been revised and improved to promote education based on respect for the individual.

Authorized Textbooks

The School Education Law requires that all elementary, middle and high schools, as well as special education schools, use textbooks that are either authorized by the Education Ministry or published under the ministry's copyright. This system is designed to ensure equality of opportunity in education, proper content of textbooks for use in the classroom, and improvement of educational standards nationwide.

Unlike the pre-war state-compiled textbook system, the current system allows private publishers to write and edit textbooks, but these must be submitted to the ministry for approval before they can be used in schools. Non-approved textbooks are not used at schools, but can be sold at bookstores. Textbook authors and publishers claim that the state-authorized textbooks system is a violation of Clause II, Article 21, of the Constitution of Japan: "No censorship shall be maintained, nor shall the secrecy of any means of communication be violated." However the Supreme Court upholds the legality of the textbook authorization system.

As part of the authorization process, the Education Ministry takes into account the expert recommendations from the Textbook Authorization and Research Council, which works in accordance with the ministry's guidelines. Each local prefecture (the administrative subdivision between national and municipal levels) or municipality board examines and adopts its own selection of authorized textbooks according to local needs. The books are distributed at the beginning of each school year. In fiscal 1994, 177.96 million copies of 1,479 titles were published and distributed.

Local Boards of Education

Cooperation between the Education Ministry and local boards of education allows the ministry to collect ample information on schools and local communities for the planning and drafting of national education policies. Local boards have to comply with these policies and with the ministry's official notices.

In line with the Education Ministry's advice on policies for administration, local boards of education execute training programs for their members, and hold conferences on issues such as revitalization of the boards and introduction of new education policies. The exchange of opinions among boards in different regions is encouraged. The ministry recommends that local boards hire capable personnel as board members and administrators, and that these employees should receive attractive salaries. Boards are also charged with improving management systems and deciding on policies that take into account the will of the local communities.

17

School Districts

Local boards of education fix school districts for public elementary and middle schools, and require that children attend the schools to which they are assigned, unless they attend a private school. Parents are rarely allowed to choose a school outside the district or to change the school to which their child is assigned. Local school officials state that all public schools provide the same level of education based on the national curriculum and authorized textbooks, so that children do not need to change schools in order to get a better education.

In January 1997, however, the Education Ministry advised municipal boards to be flexible in their administration of the school district system. Henceforth, children would be allowed to go to schools outside the districts if local boards approved the applications, and they would be permitted to change schools for reasons such as bullying, violence, or health problems.

The School Year

The Japanese school year runs from April to March. There are three terms: spring, fall, and winter. The spring term starts in early April and usually ends on July 20; after 40 days of summer vacation, the fall term starts on September 1 and finishes in mid-December; winter term begins in early January and ends in mid-March. Students living in the northern part of Japan have a shorter summer holiday and a longer winter break because of the heavy snow in that area. Summer vacations are not completely free; teachers and children have to attend several days of school during the break.

Children used to go to school six days a week, 240 days a year, with Saturday classes ending at 12:30 p.m. The shift toward the five-day week for employees allowed the Education Ministry to introduce the five-day school week in order to cut children's workload. From September 1992, the second Saturday of every month became a school holiday; in the 1995 school year, this was extended to the fourth Saturday of every month. The government has recently instructed certain schools to adopt the complete five-day school week as an experiment. Elementary and middle schools will adopt the five-day week in 2002, with high schools following suit in 2003. Even so, students will still attend school on about 200 days a year - more than the 180 days a year in American schools.

The Classroom

Most learning in Japanese schools takes place in the homeroom classroom. Students have few elective courses, and therefore only need to move out of their homeroom for laboratory sciences, music, studio art, physical education and other activities requiring special facilities.

Class size in Japan averages 36-40 students to one teacher in urban areas. This is in sharp contrast to the American average of 25-30 students per teacher; however the quiet demeanor of Japanese students and the discipline imposed on them ensure that the larger class size causes few problems.

The standard unit hour per subject in Japan is 45 minutes in elementary schools, and 50 minutes in middle and high schools. Teachers give full unit hour lectures, whilst the students copy into their notebooks all the notes on the blackboard. There is little discussion in class. High test scores are gained by students' memorization of the factual knowledge copied into their notebooks.

Teachers

The outcome of school education depends largely on the quality of teaching. In order to improve and maintain the quality of teaching in schools nationwide, the Education Ministry has established the standardized teacher-training curriculum, with which education departments in universities have to comply. This national curriculum is constantly revised by the Teacher Training Council, an advisory panel to the ministry. In accordance with the provisions of the Education Personnel Certification Law, trainee teachers are awarded their teaching certificates upon successful completion of the required subjects on their university course. Depending on the subject areas in which they plan to specialize, prospective middle and high school teachers are awarded certificates of math, Japanese, English, social studies, science, etc. There are also special certificates and temporary certificates.

The special lecturer system allows those without formal teaching certificates, but with plenty of social experience and sufficient knowledge and skills, to be appointed as special teachers for the promotion of various educational activities. In the 1997 school year, there were 141 such part-time teachers in elementary schools, and 470 in middle schools.

In addition to the initial teacher training, the Education Ministry and school boards also run many study programs for newly appointed teachers. All newly qualified teachers in elementary, middle and high schools, and in special schools for the disabled, are required to undergo a year of induction training under the guidance of a master teacher at a prefectural or municipal education center, while at the same time engaging in teaching and other educational activities in their schools. Teachers receive about two days a week of in-school training, which covers all aspects of the teacher's work: instruction, class management, preparation of report cards and other records, sponsorship of extracurricular club activities, management of physical education equipment, understanding child psychology and student guidance. There is also one day a week of out-of-school training, which includes lectures, seminars, and skill practice at education centers and other facilities. New teachers also visit other educational institutions, and participate in social-service activities, company activities and outdoor activities. During summer vacation, they attend residential workshops for about five days. The Education Ministry also runs training programs for experienced teachers, and administrative personnel.

In order to attract able students to the teaching profession, and thus improve the standard of education, it is necessary to offer a high salary. The 1974 Law Governing Special Measures on Salaries of National and Local Public School Educational Personnel guarantees better pay for public school teachers than for other public employees. In order to maintain teachers' higher salaries nationwide, the central government pays one half of the money from the national treasury in compliance with the law determining the budget for the overall standard distribution of teachers. This system allows poor local governments to employ the necessary number of teachers without being affected by their local financial situation. Furthermore, as long as the budget permits, a class can be taught by two teachers.

Moral Education

"Since education is the process of character formation, moral education can be regarded as a fundamental part of school education." (Education Ministry White Paper, 1994)

Moral education aims to prevent problem behavior such as bullying, truancy and school violence, and to encourage in children a respect for human life. It does so by fostering the development of healthy human relations, which have gradually been damaged by social changes such as the trend toward nuclear families or fewer children per household. The 1989 revised Courses of Study

23

enhanced the content of moral education by improving educational guidance and restructuring and prioritizing teaching content.

In fiscal 1993 the Education Ministry conducted an extensive survey on the implementation of moral education under the new Courses of Study, cooperating with local boards of education and public and private elementary and middle schools across the country. The survey found that almost all elementary and middle schools incorporated the subject of "moral education" into the curriculum and used supplementary books on morality.

Special Education

Special education is intended to meet the needs of physically or mentally disabled children by providing an educational environment appropriate to the type and degree of their disability, their stage of development, and their special characteristics. It helps them develop to their full potential and participate actively and independently in social activities.

Special schools are of five types: schools for the blind, the deaf, the mentally retarded, the physically handicapped, and the health impaired. The schools comprise kindergarten, elementary school, middle school, and high school departments. In high school departments, students take vocation-related subjects, an

24

enhancement of the curriculum under the new Courses of Study. As of May 1994, there were 168,239 elementary, middle and high school students in receipt of special education, approximately one percent of all students in this age bracket. According to an Education Ministry report, in fiscal 1996 there were 978 schools for the disabled, with about 86,000 children in attendance.

Children with mild disabilities can attend special classes in regular elementary or middle schools. Special classes are classified into seven types: classes for the mentally retarded, the physically handicapped, the health impaired, the visually handicapped, the hearing impaired, the speech handicapped, and the emotionally disturbed. Until 1993, disabled children were not allowed to attend subjects in a standard classroom, as it was thought that this might impede the learning of the other children. In January 1993 the enforcement regulations of the School Education Law were amended, and in April of that year a program was introduced permitting them to take classes in a normal classroom appropriate to the degree of their disability. Disabled children can now alternate between the standard classroom where they take standard subjects, and the special classroom where they receive special instruction. They can also receive special support services in resource rooms.

Physical and Health Education, and School Lunch

Physical education plays an important role in the improvement of children's health and physical fitness. Schools offer sporting activities to enhance the balanced development of children's minds and bodies. The Education Ministry provides schools with instruction manuals and videotapes for sports, and creates training and lecture programs for physical education instructors. The ministry also helps local boards of education to conduct projects such as the employment of outside instructors. Through these measures, children are expected to learn to appreciate sports, and to participate in sporting activities.

The Education Ministry has revised the Safety Guidance Handbook for Elementary Schools, to promote safety instruction in accordance with the new Courses of Study. Schools carry out care services programs such as medical examinations, environmental hygiene tests, AIDS education and safety tests for physical facilities and equipment. A guidance program for the prevention of smoking, drinking, and drug abuse is also conducted.

In elementary and middle schools, the school lunch program is included within health education. School meals are provided on all weekdays, and are intended to promote the maintenance of balanced diets and the prevention of dietary problems such as obesity. In fiscal 1992 the Education Ministry revised the Handbook on School Lunch Instruction, and since fiscal 1993, school nutritionists have undergone special training programs to improve the nutritional content of meals and the methods of preparation. The ministry also proposed the diversification of meal content: whereas traditionally, schools have provided all children with the same dish, some schools now offer multiple-choice menus or buffet-style lunches. In May 1993, school lunches were served to approximately 12.87 million schoolchildren across the country.

The Education Ministry particularly promotes meals based on rice - Japan's traditional staple food. The rice-based school lunch program started in earnest in fiscal 1986, and in fiscal 1993, rice-based meals were provided 2.6 times per week on average. The ministry claims that the program improves children's eating habits by teaching them the importance of rice. However it should also be pointed out that the ruling Liberal Democratic Party, which relies on the electoral support of rice farmers, is putting pressure on the government to boost domestic demand for rice amid the liberalization of Japan's rice market to the United States and other countries.

State Funding

The centralized Japanese education system is reflected in the centralized sources of education funding. Under this system, the ministry can control local boards of education and schools by means of distribution of the state budget. Central government distributes its education funds evenly across the country, so that remote regions are provided with equal equipment and teachers. According to an Education Ministry survey, in fiscal 1994 public expenditure on education amounted to approximately ¥9,3 trillion ($74.6 billion) from the national government and ¥13,7 trillion ($109.8 billion) from local governments: ¥17.8 trillion ($142.8 billion) was allocated to school education, ¥2.7 trillion ($21.7 billion) to social education and ¥2.5 trillion ($19.9 billion) to administrative education.

School Buildings

Many concrete school buildings built in the 1950s and 1960s are deteriorating with age. In order to improve public school facilities the Education Ministry has been promoting the construction of new buildings and gymnasiums, as well as the renovation of old buildings. In accordance with the law concerning the National Treasury's Share of Compulsory School Construction, the ministry subsidizes one half of the construction of new or additional buildings for local public compulsory schools, and one third of total expenditures for the reconstruction of buildings. In fiscal 1993, the average floor space of school buildings per schoolchild was 9.9 square meters, an increase of approximately 60 % since 1973. In the fiscal 1997 budget, ¥187.8 billion (about $1.5 billion) was paid for the construction of local public school buildings.

Private Schools and School Expenses

Approximately 80 % of kindergarten children and university and junior college students, and about 30 % of high school students, are enrolled in private schools. Although there are relatively few private elementary and middle schools, private schools have contributed to the development of education with their own school policies, including the creation of their own curricula. The Education Ministry improves educational and research conditions in private schools and eases the financial burden on students and parents. In accordance with the Private School Promotion Subsidy Law, the ministry implements a variety of measures: subsidies for private schools; long-term, low-interest loans from the Japan Private School Promotion Foundation; and favorable taxation. In fiscal 1998, ¥74.8 billion ($598.4 million) was granted to private high schools, and ¥295 billion ($2.36 billion) to private universities.

The cost to the student is higher for private school education than for public education. For example, in the 1998 school year, students in public high schools run by Tochigi Prefecture pay ¥8,700 ($69.6) for monthly tuition, and there is no entrance fee. In contrast, students at Sakushingakuin, a private high school in the Tochigi Prefecture, pay an entrance fee of ¥120,000 ($960), ¥26,000 ($208) monthly for tuition, and ¥5,000 ($40) monthly for facilities and equipment and other necessary expenses.

Educational Expenditures by Parents in Fiscal 1994 (yen)

	Kindergarten	Elementary School	Middle School	High School
Students in Public Institutions	119,728 ($958)	58,799 ($470)	136,668 ($1,093)	316,959 ($2,536)
Students in Private Institutions	297,466 ($2,380)	*	*	714,726 ($5,718)

Chapter 2: Kindergartens

Kindergartens are non-compulsory educational institutions that provide children with both fun and learning activities. The Education Ministry promotes kindergarten education to enable children to become accustomed to group activities before they enter elementary school. It has therefore increased the number of kindergartens to ensure that there is adequate provision throughout the country. In the 1996 school year, there were 14,790 kindergartens in Japan; of the 1,798,051 children attending, around 27 % were three-year olds, 57 % four-year-olds and 63 % five-year old children.

Nursery schools offer instruction similar to that provided in kindergartens. According to a survey by the Health and Welfare Ministry, in fiscal 1997 there were about 22,000 nursery schools, with provision for about 1,61 million children.

The kindergarten curriculum is set by the Kindergarten Education Conference. Its mid-term report, submitted in June 1997, emphasizes the promotion of day-care service, experience-based learning activities, health education, basic discipline for the cultivation of humanity, and cooperation with local communities. Based on the curriculum, each kindergarten sets its own daily

31

schedule and school events, offering a variety of basic studies programs (math - addition and subtraction, Japanese, etc.) and fun activities such as outings to nearby parks or museums, word games, drawing and studio arts, and athletic or cultural events. Although children are scolded if necessary, discipline is relatively lax. The aim is to let children enjoy various learning activities in a relaxed atmosphere, and thus encourage regular attendance. This stage of education familiarizes children with the learning process, group activities and group discipline, thereby easing transition to elementary school education. Children who attend kindergarten tend to be more disciplined, and more ready for actual study.

In accordance with the new Course of Study for Kindergartens, implemented in fiscal 1990, the Education Ministry has been improving instructional systems in kindergartens. It creates teachers' reference materials, and runs courses and seminars. Since fiscal 1993, mid-career teachers have been able to attend kindergarten teacher training programs, and since fiscal 1994, principals and other experienced teachers have been taking special training courses.

Chapter 3: Elementary Schools

Elementary schools represent the first stage of compulsory education, providing children with the basic knowledge necessary to begin their middle school studies. The combination of learning and fun activities offered in the schools tends to create a good educational environment, and to reduce truancy.

Within elementary school education, there is no distinction between discipline and education. Teachers believe that disciplining children at an early age helps them develop good study habits, and prevents the development of undesirable behaviors. Children are scolded when they do not follow the teachers' instructions or school rules.

Discipline and Studies

For first and second graders, discipline is stressed more than studies. Children are not allowed to make noise during class, disturb other students or run in hallways. This helps them to make the transition from kindergarten to school, and to learn that school is a place in which to study. The process is eased by the homeroom teacher system, whereby each class has its own teacher, who instructs students in all subjects. The teacher comes to know each child well, and is able to give a large amount of individual attention, and to earn the trust of his or her pupils.

In the third and fourth grades, the material studied becomes progressively more difficult. For example, in geography, children begin by learning about their own town or city. They go on to study less familiar material, concerning their prefecture for example; and then in the final two years of elementary school they will study the least familiar: the geography of Japan and the world. This process of study, in which students move gradually from the familiar to the unfamiliar, also has the effect of encouraging regular attendance and reducing truancy.

In the final two years at elementary school, specialist teachers take over from homeroom teachers for music and physical exercise. In middle and high schools, every subject is taught by a specialist.

School Ceremonies

On the first day of the spring, fall and winter term, an opening ceremony is held in the school gymnasium. Students quietly line up and sit down under the direction of their homeroom teacher. They must remain silent and take care not to disturb the line or to slouch. First, *Hinomaru,* the Japanese national flag, is hoisted in a solemn atmosphere; then children stand to sing *Kimigayo,* the national anthem, the school song and the others. Then the principal, vice principal and other teachers in charge step onto the platform one-by-one and make speeches, primarily on discipline and school rules. They praise their school for its historical background, fine educational equipment, superior personnel and excellent teaching methods. Before each speech, children must stand and bow to the speaker. Listening to the speeches, they become aware of the importance of discipline and the value of education. After the ceremony, children return to their classroom, where their homeroom teacher talks to them about class and term schedules and repeats the importance of obedience to school rules. There are no lessons, and school closes before noon.

At the end of each term children attend a closing ceremony, at which the principal and other teachers warn them against the lax discipline to which they may become accustomed during the vacation. Again, there are no classes, and after receiving a report card, children go home.

In early April new pupils and their parents attend the entrance ceremony in the gymnasium. They are greeted with applause from the teachers and other children, and then officially welcomed in a speech by the principal, who also talks about the importance of discipline and school attendance.

In mid-March sixth graders attend the commencement, which is held a few days before the closing ceremony. They enter the gymnasium to music by a children's band, receiving flowers from students in the lower grades. There are songs, and then the principal congratulates them on the completion of the first half of their compulsory education and encourages them to do well in middle school. Since middle schools demand that students spend more time on their studies, the principal urges them to discipline themselves, so they will be able to keep pace. Every child then receives an elementary school graduation certificate. Often, girls are moved to tears because they will miss their classmates and the school where they have studied for six years. When they return to the classroom, their homeroom teacher gives them their last report cards, and the class is dismissed. Similar school ceremonies are held in middle and high schools.

The Daily Schedule

A typical day in elementary school begins at 8:30 a.m. Children living in the same district gather at a designated place and leave for school in small groups of 5-10, headed by an older child (sixth grader). This system deters kidnappers. Since young children are apt to listen to people whom they do not know, the homeroom teacher constantly reinforces the message not to follow strangers.

Once at school, most children play with their friends or run around the playground. At 8.40 a.m. they line up for the morning assembly, which takes place in the playground or in the gymnasium if it is wet. Children must bow to the school principal and take care not to disturb the line. They listen quietly whilst the principal or other school officials make speeches and announcements concerning school events, or award certificates of merit.

After assembly children return to their classroom, where the homeroom teacher takes attendance and makes announcements regarding the daily schedule, studies and school rules. Morning lessons begin at 9:00 a.m., and comprise four 45 minute sessions, with a 10-minute break between each lesson.

School lunch is served at 12:30p.m. Children pay a small fee for dishes of rice, miso soup, fish, chicken, eggs, etc., which are usually eaten in the homeroom classroom. There are no cafeterias in Japanese schools. On Saturdays there is no school lunch provided, and children bring their *bento* (box lunch). Mothers have to put a great deal of time and effort into the contents of these, as there is competition between the children.

Most children eat their food quickly, in the first 10 minutes of the 40-minute lunch period; then they go to the playground or the gym for sports such as soccer, badminton, table tennis, dodge ball (the most popular for boys) and jump rope (the most popular for girls). Younger children play hide-and-seek. Some children remain in the classroom, with boys playing card games and girls playing cat's cradle or folding paper. Girls use different colored papers to create small paper cranes, 2-4 inches in height.

At 1:10 p.m. children return to class and carry out a school cleaning: they sweep the hallway and classroom thoroughly, moving all desks and chairs; they clean chalkboards, chalk and erasers, empty trashcans, clean restrooms and pick up trash from the school grounds. The hard floor is waxed once a week. Several children are assigned to clean the teacher's room; teachers themselves do not do this.

Afternoon lessons begin at 1:40 p.m. The first, second and third graders go home after one lesson, but the other students continue to study until 3:20 p.m. After school, some children play sports on the playground, and the rest go home. Children must not loiter on the way home; they are prohibited from going into the busy streets and spending money at arcades.

After Class Activities

In the summer, boys living in the countryside enjoy bicycle outings; they go to small brooks to catch crawfish and crabs, or to the mountains to catch beetles. Such activities are so popular that boys compete with each other in catching as many insects as possible. Girls' activities involve playing with peers or dolls. However children in urban areas have little access to nature, and it is dangerous to ride bicycles due to heavy traffic. Moreover, the air is so dirty and the playgrounds so small that children are discouraged from going out. Instead they stay home and spend time watching TV or playing Nintendo computer games. Computer games are so popular that millions of children spend a considerable amount of money on software and may be addicted to the games. City children spend on average half an hour listening to the radio and an hour reading, but less than half an hour per day in social relations with peers outside of school.

Example Class Schedule for Fifth Graders in the 1998 School Year

	Monday	Tuesday	Wednes-day	Thursday	Friday	Satur-day
8:30-8:40	Teachers' Meeting					
8:40-8:50	Morning Gathering					
8:50-9:00	Calling of the Roll and Announcement by the Homeroom Teacher					
9:00-9:45	Japanese	Math	Science	Drawing and Studio Arts	Japanese	Japanese
9:55-10:40	Math	Japanese			Math	Math
10:50-11:35	Social Studies	Music	Math	Japanese	Home Economics	Japanese
11:45-12:30		Science	Social Studies	Physical Ex		*
12:30-1:10	Lunch					*
1:10-1:30	School Cleaning					*
1:40-2:25	Music	Moral Education	Physical Ex	Homeroom	Health education	*
2:35-3:20	Individual Counseling	Compulsory Club Activities	*	Children's Council	Special Activities	*

Social studies and science classes emphasize exploratory activities and hands-on learning activities to develop problem-solving abilities. In home economics, children learn nutrition, cooking, sewing and other related household matters. Moral education classes use stories to encourage children to think about right and wrong. Health education covers physical growth, nutrition, AIDS, road safety, first aid and so forth. During the homeroom hour discussions are held on selected topics, and in special activities class the homeroom teacher decides on activities such as reading. The class president or vice president attends the children's council.

The class schedule does not differ significantly between schools. In middle and high schools, the schedule is tighter and more demanding, with students taking six lessons a day on Monday through Friday and four lessons on Saturday. Elementary and middle school students can choose neither subjects nor teachers; they must attend designated classes with designated teachers. High school students are allowed a few elective courses.

Sample Math Calculations Grade by Grade

	Material	Example
First Grade	Addition and Subtraction	12 + 3, 19 - 5, 10 + 8 - 6
Second Grade	Multiplication	2 × 9, 4 × 7, 68 + 29, 81 - 39, 194 + 306, 538 - 129
Third Grade	Division and Decimal	96/4, 728/7, 1.9 + 1.7, 1.3 - 0.7 + 5.6, 42 × 3 743 × 96, 1,367 + 5312 + 3,346, 50,066 - 19,994
Fourth Grade	Fraction	5/7 + 4/7, 7/9 - 2/9 - 4/9, 0.034 × 39, 1.25 × 80 70 - (34 + 26), 32 - (40 - 8 × 4), 2.7/12, 51/60
Fifth Grade	Fraction	1/2 + 1/3 + 1/4, 7/8 - 3/4, 3.2(7/2 - 2.5)
Sixth Grade	Simple Equation	64 - x - 33 = 16, 56 - 7x = 35, 1.08 + 4/15 - 0.68
Seventh Grade	Exponent and Algebra	$0.2 - (-3)^2 + 2^2, -4^2/(-4)^2$ $2(x + 1/6)/3 = 1/2, (y + 6)/3 - (y - 2)/4 = 0$ If a = -4, b = 6, calculate $-a^2 + 3b$, b/a + a/b
Eighth Grade	Simultaneous Equation	$-8x - 5y = 2$ $0.8x - 0.3y = 0.9$ $3x - 2y = 7$ $y/2 = x/6 + 2$ Simplify $-21xy^2/7y$, $8a^3b/4a^2b$, $(-x/3)^3/ (x/2)^3$ If a = 2, b = -3, calculate $(4a^2b + 6ab^2)/2ab$
Ninth Grade	Factorization, Quadratic Equation and Square Root	$x^2 + 9x + 14 = 0, (x - 2)^2 + 5(x - 2) - 6 = 0$ $x^2 - y^2 + x^2y^2 - 1 = 0, (3x + 2)(x - 4) = (x - 4)^2$ If x + y = 3, xy = -4, calculate $x^2 + y^2$ $\sqrt{32} + \sqrt{8}, \sqrt{48} - 6/\sqrt{27} + 6(-2)$
Tenth Grade	Trigonometry	If sinè + cosè = 1/3, calculate sinè/cosè + cosè/sinè, tan²è + 1/(tan²è) Simplify cosè/(1 + sinè) + cosè/(1 - sinè)

In public schools, all students in the same grade study the same material almost simultaneously nationwide. Children are not allowed to use calculators in math tests.

Teaching Guidelines and State-Authorized Textbooks

A school's class schedules are based on the national curriculum determined by the Education Ministry. Teachers are required to follow the ministry's stipulations on course selection and content for each grade level and subject. For example, in a math class for first graders, instructors must teach addition and subtraction but not multiplication, the teaching material for the second graders. In a natural science class, the teacher should not let second graders observe the growth of sunflowers, as this is material for the third grade. In this way, students in the same grade across the country learn the same subject matter, thereby ensuring quality and standardized education nationwide.

Textbooks are written in line with ministry guidelines, and must be submitted to the Education Ministry for approval before they can be used in schools. Teachers are supposed to teach only the content of the textbooks, and must cover the textbooks from beginning to end: they are not allowed to be selective. All classes in a certain grade follow the same textbook at the same rate, so if a class is cancelled for any reason, teachers have to make up for the delay by working harder. The knowledge set out in the textbooks forms the basis of homework, tests, and quizzes, and children are required to memorize it through rote learning.

Some education analysts argue that Japan's standardized curriculum demands too much study and prevents children from developing creativity, individuality and independent thinking. They insist that children should be inspired to study on their own initiative, since education is, in the first place, the process of acquiring knowledge and of developing the powers of reasoning and judgment. It is primarily a means to enrich one's mind, not the memorization of factual knowledge.

Teaching Methods

The rigid teaching schedule and large quantities of teaching materials force instructors to spend most of their classroom time giving lectures and writing on the blackboard. Children copy down what the teacher says into their notebooks, and memorize the facts and figures. Teachers rarely hold discussions in class, and children hardly ever raise their hands to express their opinions. When teachers do ask questions quick learners respond, but slow learners hesitate to speak since errors are considered to bring dishonor. Tests examine factual knowledge rather than analytical abilities.

Commercially published drill books and practice tests conform to authorized textbooks and are used to supplement these in class. Drill books contain a series of questions arranged according to their relative difficulty. As such they benefit all children in the class. Easy questions help slow learners comprehend the lecture and may deter them skipping class. For average ability children, difficult questions are a challenge to their potential. Quick learners are kept interested by the more complicated questions. Both drill books and practice tests are used to improve test scores.

Tests take place on a regular basis. Liberal-minded instructors doubt the value of testing, and argue instead that education should help to develop children's creativity and individuality. However in Japan this is difficult to achieve, for the dense national curriculum inevitably obliges teachers to teach to the tests. Most teachers use commercially published tests, which are well-written and organized, consisting of easy, average and difficult questions. Tests developed by teachers may be too easy, and thus the children's full potential will not be tested or developed. Furthermore, when tests are too easy, children stop paying attention to the lesson, neglect homework and may skip class. On the other hand, tests that are too difficult tend to demotivate all but the brightest of children.

Children are required to do homework almost every day, usually in the form of commercially published exercise sheets or home tests. Homework is intended to foster good study habits, and allows children to acquire the educational foundation necessary for success in middle and high schools.

The Report Card

At the end of each term, children receive a report card containing scholastic and attendance records, behavior and personality records, records of sports, cultural, social, volunteer activities, and teacher's comments. Scholastic records are the most important, and often list not only grades but also each child's test scores and ranking in the class. Children with good grades are happy, while those with lower grades will be reluctant to give their cards to their parents, who may scold them rather than encouraging them to do better next time. The report card encourages children to study hard and indicates their weak subjects requiring more study, but it is usually used to identify quick learners as "winners (superior)" and slow learners as "losers (inferior)." This damages the self-esteem of low-performing students, and their inferiority complex causes problems such as bullying and refusal to go to school.

Behavior and personality records are determined at the discretion of the homeroom teacher. Disobedience or other bad behavior is recorded, but children who obey school rules are

46

praised by the teacher. In this regard, behavior and personality records can help to deter children from causing trouble at school.

The Japanese report card is unique in that it judges and classifies children by merit. In the United States, the report card simply describes what each child is doing at school; it does not give the student's ranking in the class. In Denmark, there are neither report cards nor tests until the seventh grade. Japanese educators may need to discuss whether or not a report card that stresses scholastic achievement is necessary in elementary school.

Group Activities

At the beginning of each term, the homeroom teacher puts children into teams of four or five. This team grouping is intended to nurture children's cooperative spirit in activities both in and out of the classroom. In class, children are instructed to work in small groups to finish academic tasks such as summarizing a textbook; outside class time, one team might administer the class library, while another helps to prepare school meals and yet another takes care of flowerpots in the classroom and flowerbeds on the playground. A group in charge of health contacts a school nurse for regular health check-ups.

Each group selects its leader and carries out its tasks on its own initiative. The teacher scolds a lazy group and helps those who need assistance. Quick learners are usually elected leaders; they have more say than the other participants, and resolve any disputes. Other group members tend to be quiet, and are apt to obey the will of the group. The excessive dependency on the leader, and the passivity of the majority of the participants do not nurture individual creativity, but the unequal relationship among members is overlooked by the teacher, who emphasizes group spirit above the development of originality.

Japan's group-based school education is related to its cultural habit of stressing smooth assimilation into groups, in which all participants are supposed to do the same thing under the same conditions. Group members listen to their leaders and shy away from standing out, for "A tall tree catches much wind," to quote a famous Japanese proverb.

The Class President

At the beginning of each school year a class president and vice president are elected. This is intended to prevent children from relying totally on the homeroom teacher for class administration. All children are qualified to run for the presidency, but in most cases bright children run for office, or the homeroom teacher nominates a few quick learners as suitable candidates. Slow learners are reluctant to run, because they are regarded by their peers as inferior.

The class president and vice-president cooperate with the homeroom teacher on extracurricular class activities and preside over the children's council. In homeroom hour debates they often assume the roles of chairperson and secretary respectively, and lead the discussion of a given topic. However most children remain quiet in debates, and the teacher soon intervenes to lead the discussion. The children's council is also idle, showing little autonomy.

Class presidency and students' associations also exist in middle and high schools, but class representatives rely too much on teachers, who treat them like small children; as a result, they are unable to take part in school administration.

Class Size

American educators tend to criticize the large classes in Japan, arguing that children should be educated in small classes, which facilitate strong one-on-one relationships between teacher and child. However American educational values reflect American society and cannot be applied in a different cultural context. In Japan, where the students' passivity and obedience to school rules allow the teacher to concentrate on instruction based on the Education Ministry's standardized national curriculum, children learn very effectively in large classes. In 1998, the national average was 28 children per class for elementary schools and 33 for middle schools. Although classes in remote rural areas averaged only 12 children, about one-fifth of elementary schools and half of middle schools had an average of 36-40 children per class. Even so, class sizes have been reduced considerably since World War II, when classes of 60 children were normal. By 1958 the average was 50. The maximum was set at 45 in 1963 before being lowered to the current figure of 40, which was introduced for elementary and middle schools in 1980 and extended to high schools in 1993. Some local school officials have requested further reductions but the Education Ministry is content with the current figures.

Classes in the United States average 25-30. U.S President Bill Clinton's State of the Union address on January 27, 1998 proposed a further reduction.

> Now we must make our public elementary and secondary schools the world's best... raising standards, raising expectations and raising accountability... every parent already knows the key—good teachers and small classes. Tonight, I propose the first ever national effort to reduce class size in the early grades. My balanced budget will help to hire

100,000 new teachers ... with these teachers, we will actually be able to reduce class size in the first, second and third grades to an average of 18 students a class all across America.

In fact, Japanese schools have far fewer and much less serious problems than American schools with their violence, drug abuse and the high dropout rate. Self-assertive, individualistic American children can only be controlled in small classes, whereas Japanese children are quiet and assimilate themselves into the group. This reflects the marked contrast between the social and ethnic homogeneity of Japan and the heterogeneity and dynamics of the American classroom. While very few children in Japan live below the poverty line, millions of disadvantaged children in the United States, many from ethnic minorities, need more individual attention to attain their intellectual potential. This "diversity and ethnicity" means that classes must be small to promote effective learning and efficient class management, including the disciplining and motivating of problem children. In Japan, on the other hand, children are so "standardized" that they are educated and disciplined well in large classes according to a comprehensive and effective national curriculum, which contrasts with the decentralized curricula of America.

The Pecking Order

A strict hierarchy underpins the cultural homogeneity of Japan. Children obey teachers in the same way that teachers are subject to school principals, principals to local boards of education and local boards to the Education Ministry. There is no equal relationship between instructor and student - as is idealized in America - nor is there any genuine discussion between them. Teachers regard questioning by students as a challenge to their authority. Children hardly raise their hands to express their opinions in class. It is not going too far to say that teachers treat children as their subjects. Children inevitably become submissive. They must faithfully follow all the teacher's orders and the school rules exactly, or they will be scolded or even physically punished.

The teachers themselves are equally compliant towards the authorities, teaching their classes in accordance with the state curriculum in the name of the government that pays them well and secures their jobs. Since teachers enjoy high social status and respect in Japan, they never revolt against the government, unlike their American, Canadian and British counterparts, who frequently appeal to the authorities for wage hikes and improvements in working conditions.

Fun Activities

Despite the strict discipline and hierarchy, most children are satisfied with their school life and enjoy learning because the teacher provides them with interesting in- and out-of-class activities. Indeed the elementary school methodology explicitly combines study with fun activities.

When explaining material, the teacher uses pictures, folding paper, and toys, for example. In math, big dice, big colored squares or colorful cubes maintain the children's interest. In geography class, pupils learn landforms through big colored pictures or films. When they conduct a field study, they bring a packed lunch, making learning a virtual picnic.

As well as interesting curriculum-related activities, teachers organize various extra-curricular events. About once a month, children go on an excursion with their teachers to a park, hill, museum or the like, bringing a lunch along. In the summer they go swimming and in the winter go skating, or skiing in northern Japan. A cultural or music festival is held in the gym once a year when children may perform a drama or comedy, sing songs or otherwise entertain the audience. There are also fancy dress parades held on the playground when children, cheered by the crowd, wear exotic clothes from Africa or the Middle East or dress up as wizards, clowns, witches, and so on.

In the fall, the playground provides the venue for a large-scale athletic meet, held on a Saturday or Sunday before an audience of parents and other spectators. Before the event, children are permitted to practice sports and dancing almost every weekday for a month, sacrificing regular class schedules. Afternoon lessons are often cancelled for practice. At the meet itself, children are divided into two teams and compete against each other in events such as the 50 meters dash, the 1500 meters race, the 400 meters relay, an obstacle race and a tug of war. They also entertain the audience with a display of different types of dance. Parents root for their children and take pictures or videotape them. While the winning team celebrates victory, the individual winners of events are also presented with certificates of merit in front of the cheering crowd. The success of this annual event demonstrates to parents that their children are well trained athletically as well as academically, and thereby boosts the school's reputation.

Fun activities organized by the school are mandatory. Children are not allowed to skip any of these events without proper reason, nor to perform poorly on purpose, nor to stop performing. Non-compliance will result in a reprimand by the homeroom teacher. In this respect, school events not only entertain but also discipline children.

Children should think that school is a fun place, otherwise they will be reluctant to attend and learn. The teaching method in elementary education - a combination of fun activities, studies and discipline (the carrot-and-stick method), has been successful so far. Indeed, the "Survey on Attitudes towards School Education and the Five-Day School Week," conducted by a private research agency at the request of the Education Ministry in March 1994, found children's satisfaction was remarkably high. Only 8.8 % of children were displeased with school life, giving as the top three reasons "content and process of teaching and learning" (47.3 %), "friends" (41.1%) and "tests" (37.8 %). 91.2 % of elementary students were satisfied or fairly satisfied with school life. The top four reasons given were "playing and socializing with friends" (94.1 %), "school events" (71.0 %), "contact with teachers" (38.3 %) and "club activities" (35.6 %).

Perfect Attendance

On the day of commencement, prizes for perfect attendance are awarded to graduating sixth-graders who have not missed a single day of school since they first entered. In a full school assembly, the school principal hands each eligible child a certificate and a gift such as stationary and coupons for free books. The child politely receives the awards and deeply bows to the principle in a solemn atmosphere. Perhaps this ceremony reminds students in lower grades of the importance of school attendance and motivates them to get the same prizes by going to school every day. Some children are determined never to be absent from school, even if they are sick. Even so, only a few children in each school become eligible for the prizes.

The School Visitation

Twice every year, in spring and again in fall, parents are invited to visit their children's elementary and middle schools, where they can observe a class and talk to the homeroom teacher. This school visitation is, however, nothing more than an act - with both teachers and children on their best behavior, all conscious of creating the best possible impression of the school and their own abilities. Austere teachers attempt to gain favor with parents by being lenient, while even slow learners raise their hands and ask questions of the teacher.

With the exception of the school visitation days, Japanese parents rarely visit their children's schools or speak to their teachers. This is in stark contrast to the situation in America, where parental involvement is considered crucial. Take for example President Clinton 's 1998 State of the Union address:

> In the new economy, most parents work harder than ever. They face a constant struggle to balance their obligations to be good workers and their even more important obligations to be good parents. The Family and Medical Leave Act was the very first bill I was privileged to sign into law as president in 1993. Since then... about 15 million people have taken advantage of it—and I've met a lot of them all across this country. I ask you to extend that law to cover 10 million more workers and to give parents time off when they have to go see their children's teachers or take them to the doctor.

These concerns are not shared in Japan, where professionalism as regarded as far more important than parental involvement in school. Even on school visitation days, only about one-third of parents usually attend, perhaps 15 in a class of 40. Of these, approximately 90 % are mothers, usually housewives working part-time; Japanese men, who work long hours outside the home, tend to rely totally on their wives to monitor their children's education.

Nevertheless, Japanese schools function well, with fewer school problems and higher educational levels than in American schools. Indeed, the national curriculum, school rules and discipline in Japanese schools are so effective that parental involvement is not necessary to improve education.

The Home Visit

Once a year in the spring, the homeroom teacher visits each child's home to talk to parents about studies, grading, school activities and other related issues. The teacher assesses the adequacy of the educational environment in the household and advises parents on any problems the child may be having at school; however the teacher does not discuss family problems such as divorce, poverty or domestic violence. Learning about the child's home situation helps the teacher to produce a better educational plan for each child.

Parents make an effort to show that family circumstances are satisfactory for child education, but are always willing to accept the advice offered, since teachers in Japan are held in high regard and believed to be excellent educational counselors. Consequently, parents have become increasingly reliant on the school, neglecting their responsibilities as educators in the home. Fortunately this negligence does not have serious consequences, thanks to the efficiency of the Japanese school system in educating and disciplining children.

Teachers' Responsibilities for Children after School

Teachers are responsible for children both in and out of school. For example, if a child gets into trouble with the police, the homeroom teacher is sent for to sort out the mess. If a child is injured or hospitalized, his or her parents contact the teacher, even on a Sunday. Children are encouraged by their teachers to do household chores, and to find ways to help their parents. Thus, teachers take on much of the burden of parental obligations, and are blamed by parents when things go wrong. Parents fail to recognize their own responsibilities, expecting the school to provide training which ought to take place at home.

Despite the heavy responsibilities placed on them, teachers do not complain. Instead, they do their best to live up to parents' expectations. Teachers have a great deal of pride in their profession, and are happy to sacrifice their own time in order faithfully to fulfil their responsibilities. Thus they adhere to one of the important lessons in Confucianism, which has deeply influenced Japanese society.

Decline of Educational Functions in the Home

A 1993 "Opinion Survey Concerning Youth and the Family" conducted by the Public Relations Office of the Prime Minister's Office, found that 75.1 % of respondents believed that there had been a decline in the educational function of the family. The top three reasons for this were "the increasing number of parents who overprotect or spoil their children or intervene excessively in their children's lives" (64.9 %), "the increasing number of parents who take no interest in educating or disciplining their children" (35.0 %) and "reliance on outside educational institutions, such as schools and *juku* (private cram schools), for education and discipline" (33.1 %).

It is true that many parents tend to overindulge their children, believing this to be an expression of love. They adopt lax discipline, give in to their children's every whim, and do not teach them about social responsibility. Such attitudes may lead to children becoming self-centered, lazy, and disrespectful of people and authority. Misguided parents do not teach the rule of law, worrying that discipline may hurt their children's self-esteem. In truth however, submission to rules is one of our social responsibilities, and nurtures self-esteem rather than destroying it.

The consequences of lax discipline at home can be catastrophic. On April 17, 1998 the Tokyo District Court sentenced a 53-year-old man to three years in prison for murdering his 14-year-old son. The son had become increasingly violent, to the extent that his mother and sister had left home to avoid his attacks. The father remained at home to care for the boy, despite the ever-worsening violence: the boy would attack him when any request was not granted. The father sought professional help, and was advised by psychiatrists not to fight back, but to attempt to reach a "peaceful settlement." In fact, this surrender reduced a proper parent-child relationship to a ruler-ruled relationship. Finally, under extreme psychological stress, the father could take no more: he killed his son, hitting him with a metal bat and strangling him with a jump rope.

In retrospect, it is clear that the father submitted to the son in order to avoid conflicts, but in doing so, he was exploited by the son who took advantage of his weakness. Some education analysts blamed him for his conciliatory attitude, saying that if he had stood firm against the son, his family would not have broken down and a homicide would not have occurred. Yet the father's appeasement came as no surprise to most Japanese people, who tend to prefer submission or endurance to confrontation that may lead to serious domestic violence.

While the case cited above is extreme, the problems of weak home discipline are widespread throughout Japanese society. A 1997 survey by the Japan Youth Research Institute revealed that 37.9 % of middle school students did not respect their parents, 55.1 % often disobeyed their parents, 30.9 % did not want to take care of their aging parents in the future and 63.4 % believed that laws and regulations were often harmful to their interests. The same attitudes were found among high school students.

This should not be taken to suggest that parents do not care about their children's upbringing. A 1994 Education Ministry "Survey on Attitudes to School Education and the Five-Day School Week" asked parents to "list the qualities that they most wanted to instill in their children." Responses included "consideration for others" (84.1 %), "basic life skills" (76.7 %), "autonomy and independence" (72.0 %), "a sense of responsibility" (70.8 %), "a cheerful and open disposition" (66.1 %) and "justice and fairness" (55.3 %). Asked if they needed to discipline their children, 63.3 % of parents regarded discipline as "primarily the role of the family" and 24.6 % said "all things considered, it is the role of the family."

The decline of educational roles in the home is partly explained by sociological factors. A typical Japanese *salaryman* (office worker) works long hours, and does not return home until after his children have fallen asleep. At weekends, he stays home to watch TV or goes out to play golf, so he has little time to spend with his children. Without a positive male role model, boys are easily influenced by the bad behavior of their peers, and may imitate the violence and anti-social behavior that they see on TV or in the movies. Moreover, when this happens, there is no effective male discipline.

Home Training and Non-Corporal Punishment

While many parents are too lenient, some tend to the opposite extreme and use corporal punishment to discipline their children. This can be as damaging as parental neglect: children are intimidated into 'good' behavior, but may come to hate their parents, and may compensate for their own pain by bullying weaker children. However some parents do manage to strike the right balance: they teach their children the basic rules of life and discipline with non-corporal punishment, for example time-outs and loss of privileges. Such punishments are more effective than beatings, and are more likely to instill a sense of personal responsibility.

According to an Education Ministry White Paper (1994),

> It is said that character formation begins with parent-child interaction and that, above all, children need to feel loved

and to feel that their environment is peaceful. The provision of timely and appropriate discipline as part of family interaction plays a crucial role in education in the home. Indeed, education in the home can be regarded as the foundation of all education.

Thus, parents are responsible for educating children in the home, since the home is the "first school." If parents are to carry out this function, there must be a proper combination of love and discipline based on a strong one-on-one relationship between parent and child. Children have no respect for parents who overprotect them or who beat them up for their bad behavior, but ultimately appreciate parents who rectify their wrongdoing by administering non-corporal punishments. Children realize sooner or later that their parents scold them, not because they dislike them, but because discipline is an expression of love.

Community Activities

The Education Ministry White Paper (1994) stresses the educational importance of the local community:

> We must recognize that healthy human development is achieved not only through school education but also through the total life experience of children in their families and communities. And from this perspective we must correct the tendency to depend excessively on school education and work instead to ensure that schools, families, and

64

communities all play their appropriate roles in education to
the full.

Similarly, a majority of parents believe that adults' active
involvement in their communities is important to the healthy
development of children; that the more they participate in
community activities, the more children will too, because children
grow by observing adult behavior. In a 1994 Education Ministry
survey, 56.9 % of the parents polled stated that adults "should be
actively involved" and 32.4 % felt "involvement is preferable."

In reality, however, these positive responses are often
mere lip service. Men inevitably put the highest priority on their
profession and give little consideration to community involvement. If
children do copy adults, they will lose interest in community
voluntary activities. Indeed there seems to be a lack of community
spirit in students (particularly boys) reflecting the low commitment
of most adults. According to a survey conducted by the Tochigi
Comprehensive Education Center in Tochigi Prefecture on October
1997, about 70 % of the 1,200 middle and high school students
polled said that they had not participated in voluntary activities, and
nearly half of all male students "do not want to participate." More
than 80 % of female students said that they "would like to
participate" if they had the time or the opportunity.

Despite its White Paper drawing attention to the problem of extreme dependency on school education, the Education Ministry too might be accused of lip service and self-contradiction. The proposed cooperation among schools, families and communities cannot be implemented because the rigid, dense national curriculum allows little time for community activities. Teachers and parents want children to concentrate on their studies instead of "wasting time" on voluntary activities with local people. The PTA (parent-teacher association) provides children with few opportunities to participate in meaningful events such as visits to elderly people. As a result, children play with friends or play video games rather than getting involved with other people.

For children to attain a sense of moral obligation, they need real participation, not just moral theories. Moral obligation is, of course, different from compliance with school rules or laws. Children are told not to shoplift, smoke cigarettes, bully peers, play truant and the like. Most observe these rules, but that does not mean they have a community spirit. In moral education classes they are taught the distinction between right and wrong, respect for life and the importance of being kind to others, yet Japanese children rarely experience voluntary activity. Lessons in the classroom do not nurture the community spirit that is acquired through actual voluntary activities.

Volunteer Spirit

Let's take a close look at the meaning of volunteer spirit. According to the Random House Collage Dictionary (1982), the word 'volunteer' means "1. a person who offers himself for a service without obligation to do so. 2. a person who performs a service willingly and without pay." From a philosophical point of view, a volunteer does good to fulfil a sense of moral duty, which requires identification of one's own interests with the interests of others. A lack of volunteer spirit means that one's course of action is generated by self-love, which uses others only as a means to an end.

Volunteer spirit is accompanied by good will (conscience), which is itself worthy of praise; conscience guides children as to the right course of action, and discourages them from doing wrong. In this respect, it is imperative that parents, teachers and communities instill in children a sense of moral duty.

Unfortunately, however, volunteerism has not taken root in Japan. People are by and large indifferent to the hardships of the elderly and the disabled. Thus children, whose behavior is the mirror image of the adult world, do not offer help unless ordered to by their parents or teachers. Indeed, if they see a wheelchair-bound

67

person having trouble in crossing the road, they might even laugh at him or her instead of helping.

This indifference to volunteer activities is not surprising given the prevailing social attitudes in Japan. The poor and the weak, the homeless and the disabled are regarded as inferior, and ignored by the upper and middle classes. This rigid social hierarchy is so dominant and widespread throughout every aspect of Japanese life that children can not be expected to understand volunteerism, however strongly the Education Ministry or local school officials emphasize its value.

Female Teachers

In fiscal 1996 there were 262,237 female teachers in elementary schools, compared with 163,477 male teachers. Teaching is one of very few professions in Japan in which men and women receive equal pay and conditions and this, combined with women's naturally greater interest in children, is encouraging more and more women to seek jobs in school.

Female teachers tend to be more sensitive to the needs of their pupils. They are more attentive to children's behavior and their process of development, and give greater consideration to how best to help each of the children in their charge, both in and out of school. Male teachers on the other hand, tend to be concerned with children's academic performance. In other words, females tend to be more "process-oriented," while males are more "result-oriented." This makes females better suited to teaching in elementary schools, as can be seen in the different approaches to children's group activities. Female teachers often divide children into small teams and let them cooperate with each other to execute given tasks; they like to observe what each child is doing and give help if necessary. Male teachers also put children in teams, but they prefer to give a lecture and write on the blackboard, and expect children to take notes. There is little room in the latter approach for the group work that is so highly prized in elementary schools. This difference cannot be explained merely in cultural terms. Even in American schools, where there are generally fewer group activities, female teachers offer more group activities than do males. In particular, female language instructors encourage team or pair work for questions and answers or for conversation practice.

Gender Discrimination in School

Conservative Japanese society is still a long way from accepting gender equality. Even in schools, where there are so many female professionals, there are unwritten laws leading to defined gender roles. Female teachers come to school early in the morning and empty trash cans, sweep floors and clean desks; they are also expected to serve tea or coffee to their male colleagues, and to behave politely and courteously to them. This subordinate status inevitably leads to there being fewer female principals and vice principals. In 1993, only 5.0 % of principals and 10.8 % of vice principles in elementary, middle and high schools were women.

Discrimination against female teachers is a reflection of male-dominated Japanese society. Official figures show that women spend more than four hours a day performing about 90 % of uncompensated housework such as cleaning, cooking and child rearing, while men spend only about 30 minutes a day on such work. Women also work 35.1 % of paid working hours, against 64.1 % for men. If paid and unpaid work hours are combined, women work longer hours than men. Moreover, high-profile posts are less accessible to women not only in schools but throughout Japanese society. According to a 1997 White Paper on equal opportunities released by the Prime Minister's Office, women make up only 6.7 % of the Japanese Diet; while in other industrialized nations women hold 14.5 % of such positions. In Japan women occupy only 8.5 % of administrative and managerial posts, compared to 27.4 % in other industrialized nations.

Female teachers rarely protest about their inferior status, because in Japan passivity is regarded as one of the most important female attributes. Women know that nothing can be gained without it being demanded, but their excessive politeness and adherence to social convention prevent them from holding an open discussion on the issue. Consequently, female teachers set a bad example for children, and their submissive behavior reinforces the cultural norm: schoolgirls learn to accept unequal relations between the sexes and to be submissive themselves, while boys learn to take for granted male superiority. In this situation gender inequality remains steadfast in school.

Chapter 4: Middle Schools

Middle schools provide the final three years of compulsory common education, during which students are making the psychological transition from childhood to adolescence. In order to combat any antisocial or rebellious behavior in school, there is added emphasis on discipline, and children are required to wear school uniform. It is at this stage that English enters the national curriculum.

Children's Psychological Development

Adolescence begins as early as the fourth grade. The transition from childhood to adulthood is characterized by the acquisition of an intricate stream of consciousness, ranging from simple anger and joy to complex emotions such as shame and pride, and the development of empathy and conscience. Thus, adolescents can make better judgements and enjoy more freedom than elementary students whose lack of reasoning power prevents them from making independent decisions. While elementary school students depend on the protective supervision of parents and teachers to foresee and prevent accidents, middle school students

72

are allowed to play sports in the playground and to go downtown or elsewhere on their own.

Adolescents develop originality and an independent spirit. Middle school students abandon toys and seek an adult identity. Boys are no longer eager to collect insects, nor do girls want to play with dolls. Some girls begin to use makeup and dye their hair to differentiate themselves; some boys change their hairstyles and wear fashionable clothes in order to impress the opposite sex. The adolescent's pursuit of independence can be problematic however, for at that age young people are immature and still need guidance from parents and teachers. Pre-teens and teenagers tend to develop a rebellious spirit, testing limits and often coming into conflict with school rules and the law. Their quest for unrestricted freedom needs to be kept in check.

School Rules

According to the Education Ministry's White Paper (1994), school rules "enable schoolchildren to enjoy healthy school lives and achieve better growth and development. They are formulated by, and at the discretion of, individual schools." Despite this freedom, nearly all middle schools draft harsh rules. Parents support rigid discipline, and often request even stricter school regulations. Similarly, most teachers fear that adolescents' psychological development will cause problems unless checked. They believe that students who show individuality or originality in appearance and behavior are prone to protest against teachers, break school rules, get involved in stimulant drugs or commit other misdeeds; are indeed potential juvenile delinquents, a threat to school and society.

A strict school uniform policy is intended primarily to prevent students from spending too much time and money on fashionable clothing and appearance. It also discourages flirtation: teachers view dating as a waste of valuable study time, and students seen kissing or hugging are reprimanded. Perfume is prohibited, as are extravagant hairstyles. Male students in cities must have short hair and in the countryside they are required to have their hair close-cropped. Boys wear military-looking black uniforms and black school caps; girls wear sailor suits with pleated shirts, which must be worn even in winter when the temperature drops to around -10 C (12 F) north of Tokyo. Only if she makes a request to the homeroom teacher might a girl be permitted to wear trousers.

The introduction of uniforms, however, has a negative effect on the development of students' independent spirit. Students are severely reprimanded if teachers notice any modification of the

74

uniform, for example the lengthening of trousers or skirts, rolling up collars, altering buttons. Since all students look similar to each other, they are dissuaded from standing out or being rebellious. The uniform buries individuality, making it much easier for teachers to compel students to conform to school rules and execute tasks in a group activity, in which all do the same things at the same time under the same conditions. Furthermore, because the design of each school's uniform is unique, students are easily identifiable to the public when outside the school premises, which deters them from wrongdoing and from being ill-mannered. To maintain their reputations, some schools make a list of prohibited behavior in public, including spitting, eating while walking, and chewing gum.

This, of course, contrasts diametrically with the lax school dress codes in the United States, where any move to institute uniforms meets with opposition. When the board of education in New York City unanimously decided on March 18, 1998 merely to recommend that elementary schools in the district adopt uniforms as of September 1999, parents and children were divided in their opinions. The rule, which unwilling individual schools or parents were allowed to ignore, aimed to make students focus on their studies and not be distracted by their clothing. Parents and students could design the uniforms, and parents would pay somewhere between $100 and $120 per year for clothing their children. The board expected that most of its 500,000 elementary students would comply with the rule: around 70,000 students had already worn pleated skirts or navy pants, white shirts, ties, etc. in an optional uniform program. Even though the rule is not binding, critics still regard it as unacceptable government interference. The controversy exemplifies American society's sensitivity to the ideal of freedom of choice. This is very different from the Japanese priority of obedience to the authorities. While Japanese students may be displeased with the severe rules that limit their freedom and creativity, they rarely complain, recognizing their subservience in the school hierarchy. They have no choice but to follow the rules dutifully.

Corporal Punishment

Although corporal punishment is officially prohibited, students who violate school rules are often physically punished by teachers who believe that non-physical means are not enough for the complete enforcement of school rules. According to an Education Ministry survey, a record 393 teachers administered corporal punishment on children in 1996, 37.4 % higher than the previous year. Eight of the teachers were suspended; 34 had their wages cut; 68 were warned; 28 were reprimanded. A record 206 principals or head teachers were also disciplined for overlooking corporal punishment. This, however, is the tip of the iceberg. Violence by teachers is rarely detected because most victims bear the insult silently and witnesses tend to give tacit consent. Many parents tolerate teachers' decisions, believing that corporal punishment is a "necessary evil" that effectively contains and disciplines problem students. Parents trust teachers so most violence by teachers is not made public, nor is it investigated by the police, unless students are seriously injured. Teachers have little sense of guilt and are not concerned about a student's human rights. For children punishment is imposed arbitrarily and without proper proceedings, unlike criminal offenders who have a fair trial in accordance with the law.

When I was a middle school student, I often witnessed corporal punishment. One day during a music class, a female teacher asked the students to hand over their homework, but one boy forgot to bring his assignment. The enraged teacher boxed his ears. In a Japanese class, another boy was having a chat with his friend, while a male teacher was lecturing. The teacher suddenly hit the student's jaw with a bamboo sword without giving any prior warning; as a result, a little blood flowed down his neck. The student pressed on the injured part with a tissue but did not go to the school nurse. The teacher did not apologize to him and continued to give his lecture as if nothing had occurred. In retrospect, if the rule of law should be respected in schools, the incident should have been reported to the police. But the students in the class were quiet and nobody called the police, worrying about possible retaliation by the teacher who might have lowered the grades of those who accused him. As for me, when I was a ninth-grader, I was slapped by my homeroom teacher for playing forbidden computer games at a game center on the high street.

Violence by teachers occurs in elementary and high schools as well. At about 1 p.m. on April 23, 1997, a second-year student at Kumiyama High School in the Kyoto Prefecture was smoking in a restroom. A teacher on patrol detected cigarette smoke rising from a toilet stall. He questioned the student, who denied smoking and did not hand over the pack of cigarettes. The teacher carried the student in his arms and suspended him headfirst out of a third floor window, about seven meters (23 feet) above ground - this for not giving him his pack.

Corporal punishment is administered only to male students, who are more likely to violate school rules than girls. Girls are so obedient that they do not have to be threatened with penalties, and there is a tacit consensus that they should be immune from punishment. However, girls do become the objects of molestation. A survey by the Education Ministry revealed that 66 teachers were punished and 27 were dismissed for sexual abuse on elementary, middle and high school girls in fiscal 1996, a 36.5 % increase on the previous year.

In early September 1997, a 49-year-old male teacher at a public elementary school in Itami, Hyogo Prefecture, molested a female fifth grader during a school excursion. The teacher reportedly touched the girl in a students' bedroom on the fifth day of a six-day school trip. The student was so shocked that she did not attend school after the excursion. The Itami Municipal Board of Education received the case and began their investigations by summoning the teacher, who had taken extended leave just after the incident. He testified at a hearing that while he was patrolling students' bedrooms at night, he saw the girl awake on a bed, so he approached the bed and touched the student to take care of her until she fell asleep. He insisted that his act was part of the guidance he gave the girl. The teacher received an oral warning from the board of education for an "excessive act." He quit his job in March 1998 without being penalized. In the same month, the school principal was reprimanded for improper handling of the teacher's misconduct. The board of education was also criticized for allowing the teacher to leave his post without penalty.

Three factors underlie the failure to deter corporal punishment or sexual harassment. First, schools and boards of education are unwilling to inflict on teachers penalties that match their offenses. Whereas in most modern societies crime and punishment are balanced regardless of the social status of the offenders, in the hierarchical school society teachers are treated with respect by parents and communities, who implicitly exempt them from liability as long as the corporal punishment is minor. Second, local educational authorities are reluctant to make cases public and keen to protect the honor of problem teachers and the reputation of the schools. For example, only after a citzens' group protested about concealment did a board of education in Osaka inform the Education Ministry of eight corporal punishment cases in the city's schools during the 1996 academic year. Similarly, the board of education in Hyogo Prefecture attempted to conceal an incident in which a teacher injured the eye of a fifth-grader, which took a week to heal. It was not until the rumors of a cover-up spread that the town reported the case to the prefecture. Third, far from instructing local educational authorities to be responsible to the general public, the Education Ministry itself hides important facts in order to protect the accused. Information on the number of punished teachers and the dates of the incidents is available to the media, but details of individual cases are withheld despite the fact that announcement of each incident would dissuade teachers from abusing students.

Although the disclosure of information on corporal punishment is insufficient, some local school officials are taking measures to stop violence by teachers. In January 1998 the board of education of Tachikawa, western Tokyo, introduced training sessions in which teachers take on the roles of either inflicter or victim of corporal punishment. About 60 teachers of the 21 municipal elementary schools and nine middle schools participated in the two-day sessions to experience the pain that students feel when they are assaulted. If this method were adopted by all schools, violence by teachers across the country might decrease considerably. However, the measure introduced in Tachikawa is exceptional. Given the rigid hierarchy in schools, most local boards of education would not undermine the authority of teachers by making them play the role of victims.

Lax Discipline

Just as some teachers overstep the mark by administering corporal punishment, others are too lenient. In particular, young female teachers do not always scold disruptive or violent students, whom they may find difficult or impossible to deal with. They may even be intimidated, since most male ninth graders are much bigger (5'6" on average) than female teachers (5'1").

81

Lax discipline inevitably causes problems, especially to the majority of students who wish to concentrate on the lesson. For example, some male students may start playing cards or table tennis during a regular lesson in the homeroom classroom, realizing that they will not be disciplined. The teacher must stand firm against those who violate school rules. If students are reprimanded for inappropriate acts, they clearly learn right from wrong and are thereby deterred from repeating problem behavior. The teacher who fails to teach and make the distinction between good and bad behavior is treated with contempt by students.

Role Models and Morality

Teachers instruct students to observe school rules, yet they do not set a good example by their own behavior. For example, while students are obliged to take part in school cleaning, teachers have no such duty; as a result, students take this inequality for granted. Similarly, students are not allowed to smoke, yet many teachers smoke in the teachers' rooms. More seriously, some teachers set such a bad example that they betray entirely the trust invested in them as educators. On March 18, 1998 the Kobe Municipal Board of Education suspended the principal of Tomogaoka Middle School in Kobe, Hyogo Prefecture, for his visit to a strip club. A weekly magazine had revealed that the principal had visited the club after the school's graduation ceremony on March 13. The superintendent of the board of education apologized for the principal's act and regretted the incident, because it might harm the feelings of children at the school. The principal admitted to the committee that the magazine article was correct and expressed remorse for his behavior; he was ordered to remain at home for an undisclosed period. On March 19, the board of education held an emergency meeting of school principals in the city to discuss the issue.

Most education analysts were in favor of the punishment imposed on the principal, arguing that educators, who should behave in compliance with morality, should not watch topless shows, which degrade women's dignity and define them as sex objects rather than as equals. It was also claimed that teachers should behave ethically all the time to set a good example for students, or the trust between them would crumble. However some critics contended that teachers' privacy should be respected, and that they should not be blamed for activities in their free time unless those acts were illegal.

Studies and Tests

Middle school students are motivated to study long and hard so that ultimately they will pass high school entrance exams. Teachers push students to study for regular mid-term and end-of-term exams, chapter tests and several other types of tests including quizzes. A regular exam tests knowledge on all the subjects: math, Japanese, English, social studies, science, health and physical education, music, art, etc. The examination schedule is spread over a couple of days, with four or five subjects tested each day. The results count for about 80 % of the final grades.

Before the 1993 school year, a commercially produced achievement test similar in style and difficulty to an actual high school entrance exam was given several times a year to tens of thousands of students. Students who did well on the tests were almost certain to pass the exam of a top high school, but those who got bad test scores were advised to take the exam of a below-average high school. According to a survey conducted by the Education Ministry in 1992, middle schools in 44 of the nation's 47 prefectures employed the results of these tests as the guideline for the selection of high schools or for students' career guidance in the 1991 school year.

However the use of commercially produced tests meant that teaching tended to be concentrated toward the test, and competition in the high school entrance exams intensified. Thus, the Education Ministry recommended that local boards of education stop using the tests. The ministry's proposal was implemented as of the 1993 school year. Even so, there are still a number of tests at school, and students need to study every day to prepare. Average students sit at their desks at home approximately two hours per weekday and about three hours on Sunday. Some study for even longer, five or six hours a day.

The growing pressure on students to study inevitably causes dissatisfaction with school life. According to a survey conducted by the Education Ministry in March 1994, while only 8.8 % of elementary students were displeased with school life, this figure rose to 29.3 % in middle schools and 35.8 % in high schools. The top three reasons for discontent for middle school students were "one's own grades" (49.7 %), "school regulations" (48.6 %) and "teachers" (40.7 %). High school students cited "one's own grades" most frequently (53.1 %), followed by "content and process of teaching and learning" (40.2 %) and "teachers" (35.6 %). Clearly, students feel great pressure from testing, school rules and teachers.

Memorization

One of the most important methods of learning in Japanese schools is memorization of factual knowledge. Tests require students to have a large amount of factual knowledge, and so rote learning, rather than the development of analytical abilities, is crucial to doing well. Thus, in a geography class students memorize the names and capital cities of all major countries, and the location of large rivers, mountains, islands and oceans. In a world history class, students memorize important facts about the Civil War, the Emancipation Proclamation and the founding of the Ku Klux Klan, but do not analyze the reasons why these events occurred, nor do teachers explain the causes of events. Therefore, the students are learning only "unconnected facts," which are forgotten soon after the test. Certainly, analysis of the causes of historical events is not an easy task for middle and high school students, but this sort of investigation would enhance their problem-solving skills and their ability to interpret complex data.

English

English is introduced into the curriculum in middle school, and is the only foreign language taught. Students begin by learning the English alphabet, and move on to memorizing simple sentences such as "This is a pen" and "I am a student." By the time they graduate from school, they should have learned a basic 1,000 word vocabulary, and be able to read a simple text and translate simple Japanese into English, and vice versa.

However there are many difficulties with English instruction in Japan. Most teachers of English have little practical command of the language; they speak English slowly and with incorrect pronunciation and articulation, and are unable to follow English spoken at normal speed. Lacking confidence in conversation, Japanese teachers of English teach to their strengths, stressing grammar, reading and writing. Students rarely practice listening and speaking, and so even after years of study, they are unable to communicate with a native speaker.

These difficulties may be explained at least in part by the differences in pronunciation and articulation between Japanese and English. The Japanese language does not have as many sounds as English: there are only five vowels in Japanese, but sixteen in English. There is no distinction between "r" and "l" in Japanese, or between "b" and "v", so some Japanese teachers of English may say, "I rub you," instead of "I love you." The Japanese language also lacks both accents and intonation and therefore, special practice is usually necessary to pronounce English sounds correctly. It is worth pointing out that German and French students of English do not experience these problems, since English, German and French sounds are more or less similar to one another.

Nevertheless, lack of practical language education is not considered a problem in Japan, where English is taught as an "exam subject," not as a foreign language. Students are tested on grammar, reading and writing; if there is a listening comprehension section, this consists of English at unnaturally slow-speed, so that all the listeners are able to understand. This is a "new English" usable only in the classroom; no consideration is given to the use of language for practical purposes like communication with foreign people and travels abroad. Consequently, English studies at school become uninteresting and tedious, a matter of memorizing grammar and vocabulary.

Let's take a look at a high school English entrance exam. The following is part of the English exam given by Kokugakutochigi High School in Tochigi Prefecture on Jan. 30, 1998.

A. In each parenthesis, choose one of the four words whose pronunciation of its underlined part is different from the others'.

1. (a. <u>ex</u>cuse   b. <u>ex</u>ample   c. <u>ex</u>perience   d. <u>ex</u>plain)
2. (a. look<u>ed</u>   b. help<u>ed</u>   c. need<u>ed</u>   d. wash<u>ed</u>)
3. (a. c<u>ow</u>   b. t<u>ow</u>n   c. p<u>ow</u>er   d. sl<u>ow</u>   )

Answer: 1 - b, 2 - c, 3 - d

B. In each parenthesis, choose one of the four words whose position of accent is different from the others'.

1. (a. be-come   b. moun-tain   c. art-ist   d. lan-guage   )
2. (a. re-mem-ber   b. mu-si-cian   c. to-geth-er   d. un-der-stand)
3. (a. veg-e-ta-ble   b. dic-tio-nar-y   c. con-ver-sa-tion   d. in-ter-est-ing)

Answer: 1 - a, 2 - d, 3 - c

C. Choose the one of the four underlined words one stresses when reading the conversation between A and B.

1. A: Good afternoon, Roy. How are you?
   B: Very well, thank you. <u>And</u> <u>how</u> <u>are</u> <u>you</u>?
                                               a   b   c   d
2. A: Did Tom play baseball with his friends yesterday afternoon?
   B: No, he didn't. <u>He</u> <u>watched</u> it <u>with</u> <u>them</u>.
                               a   b   c   d

Answer: 1 - d, 2 - b

It is astonishing that English pronunciation and accents are examined on a written test! This type of test allows students who do not speak English at all to perform well just by memorizing pronunciation patterns from a textbook.

The following is part of a March 1998 entrance exam for Tochigi public high schools.

A. Choose an appropriate word in each parenthesis to complete the sentence.

1. Ken and I (am, are, is, was) good friends.
2. (Why, Who, Which, What) were you late today?
3. (Do, Did, Have, Has) you finished your homework yet?
4. This story (is written, was written, is writing, was writing) a long time ago.
5. Ben asked me (wait, waited, waiting, to wait) here.

Answer: 1 - are, 2 - Why, 3 - Have, 4 - was written, 5 - to wait

B. Read the following story and choose the answer to each question from a to j.

Yumi is a high school student. She is a member of the cooking club at her school. The club members bring meals to old people every month. Last Friday, after school, she cooked a meal with her club members. Then she and her friend, Sachiko, visited an old woman.

The old woman's house is near Yumi's school. She lives alone. She doesn't have many people who visit her. When Yumi and Sachiko visited her, she looked very happy. She enjoyed eating the meal with them. She also showed them some pictures and talked about her old friends.

After the girls had a good time with the old woman, Yumi said, "We must go home now, but we are going to come and see you again next month. What do you want to eat them?" The old woman answered, "I just want to talk with you. So you don't have to bring any food." "OK. I understand," said Yumi. "We'll sing some songs next time," said Sachiko. The old woman smiled and thanked them.

1. Do the club members bring meals to old people every month?
2. Who did Yumi and Sachiko visit after school last Friday?
3. Where does the old woman live?
4. What did the old woman talk about?
5. Why did the old woman say, "You don't have to bring any food"?

a. They visited an old woman living alone.
b. Near Yumi's school.
c. Because she didn't like Yumi's meal.

90

d. She talked about her job.
e. They visited an old woman and her family.
f. No, they don't.
g. She talked about her old friends.
h. She lives alone.
i. Because she just wanted to talk with the girls.
j. Yes, they do.

Answer: 1 - j, 2 - a, 3 - b, 4 - g, 5 - I

Grammar questions always appear on a test, and most questions are multiple choice, testing factual knowledge rather than thinking skills. The low level of this English entrance exam suggests that English is a difficult language for Japanese students.

The Education Ministry has been aware of the heavy bias toward grammar in English education. To improve students' practical communication skills, it introduced in fiscal 1987 the Japan Exchange and Teaching Program (JET), under which about 5,000 native speakers per year are invited to Japan as assistant English teachers working in middle and high schools across the country. In fiscal 1998, according to a Home Affairs Ministry report, local governments would invite 5,721 foreign nationals from 35 countries in line with the JET Program. Of the total, 5,123 would be hired as assistant language teachers, 552 would work for cultural exchanges at local governments and 46 would be employed for community sports events. The program has provided students with more opportunities to communicate with native speakers, and has contributed to the promotion of international understanding between Japanese and other peoples.

However, the JET Program has had only limited success in helping students to improve their foreign language conversation skills. This is because of the disproportional native English teacher-student ratio, about 1:1,815. It is impossible for one native speaker to take care of 1,815 students and improve their communication skills. At least 100,000 foreign nationals would be necessary to realize the aims of the program.

Another problem involved in the JET Program is the treatment of native speakers working as assistant English teachers. They are introduced to students as "Assistant Language Teachers (ALTs)," with the implication that they should serve their Japanese counterparts. ALTs who hope to work on an equal footing with their partners are humiliated. Japanese teachers spare little time for talks with ALTs, so constructive team teaching is virtually impossible; this is a ruler-ruled relationship undermining the mutual respect and understanding necessary for teamwork and real communication. Female ALTs tend to gain a particularly bad impression of Japanese society, being shocked not only by their treatment as assistants, but also by the extent of sexism in schools.

This lack of communication between Japanese teachers and ALTs may be explained by a number of factors. Japanese teachers are not confident engaging in English conversation and become uneasy with non-Japanese people. They are also kept extremely busy with clerical work, attending teachers' meetings, supervising extracurricular club activities and dealing with problem students, so they have little time to attend to ALTs. There is also a lack of training for the parties involved: schools do not provide Japanese teachers with training programs on how to make good use of native speakers in the classroom, and whilst ALTs undergo training to get used to the Japanese education system and society before teaching in middle or high schools, more programs are necessary for them to really understand Japan. Most importantly, however, the closed nature of Japanese schools leads Japanese teachers to treat foreign nationals unequally, as outsiders.

Along with the JET Program, the Education Ministry has also introduced an in-service training program, whereby Japanese teachers of English can attend institutions of higher education in the UK, the U.S., Australia and New Zealand to improve their English competency and language teaching methods. This program is likely to be more useful and effective: it will improve the quality of language teaching in Japanese schools without all the problems that surround the JET program.

There have been some proposals to change the system of language teaching in Japanese schools. Some education analysts for example, have been calling for language teaching to start much earlier, in elementary schools. On October 8, 1997, the Curriculum Council proposed the introduction of English education in elementary schools, to begin in the 2003 academic year. Emphasis would be placed on learning the lifestyles and cultures of the English-speaking world rather than teaching to the test. The council also proposed a change of focus in English education in middle and high schools, from grammar and reading to listening and speaking. Consideration is also being given to allowing schools to teach a foreign language other than English.

Juku, Private Cram Schools

In addition to attending regular schools, more than 60 % of students enroll in *juku*, private cram schools operating outside regular school hours. The *juku* provides students with special instruction in the evenings, and on Saturdays or Sundays until as late as 10:00 p.m.. Quick learners are offered high-level lessons on how to pass the entrance exams of top high schools, and slow learners are given supplementary lessons to catch up with their regular schoolwork. Elementary school students also enroll, to prepare for the entrance exams of private middle schools, where competition for admission is fierce. According to a survey by the

Education Ministry, the top four reasons cited by parents for sending children to *juku* were "The child wants to attend" (46.0 %), "No one at home can help with studies" (33.3 %), "The child does not study independently" (32.4 %), and "School study alone is not enough to ensure success in entrance examinations" (26.0 %).

Regular schools are inferior to *juku* in terms of teaching content and methods. For example, regular school English teachers use an authorized English textbook that limits the range of English vocabulary to about 1,000 words, which is insufficient to deal with the 2,000 word-level English exam of a renowned high school. Restrictive teaching guidelines prevent regular school teachers from introducing higher level material; they have to teach only what is written in the textbooks, and there is little motivation to improve teaching content or methods. Many teachers fall into a rut of giving dull, unchallenging lessons. This reluctance to improve is reinforced by job security in the teaching profession - public school teachers are guaranteed lifetime employment no matter how bad their teaching is.

While regular schools depend on the Education Ministry for revision of teaching content, the *juku* continuously improves its curriculum and the quality of teachers and instruction. It does not have to use authorized textbooks, nor does it have to follow the Education Ministry's teaching guidelines. Some cram schools even

95

set up video cameras in classrooms to monitor teaching quality. *Juku* instructors do not teach materials irrelevant to an entrance exam, but do teach useful question-solving techniques and efficient rote learning methods to help students answer complicated questions as quickly as possible. The trial exams given by *Juku* are often more difficult than actual entrance exams; for example, students read 2,000 word-level English sentences in an English test, so that they can easily handle a 1,500 word-level actual exam. *Juku* students learn so effectively that they are said to absorb knowledge twice as fast as they do in regular schools. Clearly, students enrolled in cram schools are at an advantage in high school entrance exams.

    Juku attendance is increasing every year. According to Education Ministry statistics, 12.0 % of elementary students were enrolled in cram schools in fiscal 1976, 16.5 % in 1985 and 23.6 % in 1993. The figures for middle school students were 38.0 % in fiscal 1976, 44.5 % in 1985 and 59.5 % in 1993. A survey by the Tokai Bank, Ltd., "Expenditure on Education for Children," found that in 1995 13.5 % of elementary students and 62.7 % of middle school students attended *Juku*; in 1996 the figures were 35.5 % and 63.6 % respectively. The latest figures, provided by the Japan Parent-Teacher Association National Conference, reveal that in December 1997, 43.1 % of sixth graders and 64.3 % of ninth graders were enrolled in cram schools. Their survey polled sixth-year elementary students, third-year middle school students and parents and teachers nationwide. Of students enrolled in cram schools, 61.7 % of sixth graders and 59.5 % of ninth graders said that they "would like to continue to attend *juku*," because their grades would improve, they could understand the lessons well or they were motivated to study. Of the sixth graders, 83.9 % said that they "enjoy *juku*." Of the ninth graders, 29.9 % "enjoy *juku*" and 47.7 % "are fairly satisfied," while 21.6 % "are not satisfied." Regarding lessons in cram schools, 82.8 % of the ninth graders said that they "understand well" or " understand fairly well," while 2.6 % "do not understand." In contrast 46.7 % of all the children polled said that they understood regular school lessons very well or fairly well, while 9.3 % did not. This shows that children learn better in *juku* than in regular schools. Forty-seven percent of ninth-graders enrolled in cram schools said that they went home about 10 P.M., and around 60 % after 10 p.m., and 44.6 % complained about fatigue due to attending *juku*.

Cram schools are businesses, and as such must attract custom, that is, students. A survey conducted by the Management and Coordination Agency in 1994 found that the number of *juku* across the country was about 47,500, with a total annual revenue of about ¥900 billion ($7.5 billion). Each student pays about ¥30,000

($250) a month on average. Competition is intense, with each cram school adopting strategies to recruit more and more students. One *juku*, the Hoshino Seminar in Maebashi City, Gunma Prefecture, offered cash prizes to its students. In October 1997 it put 50,000 inserts in the newspaper, saying that it would give prizes to its top 26 students: the top five students would receive ¥400,000 ($3,300), the next five ¥300,000 ($2,500), and so on. According to the school, students and their parents agreed with this scholarship system, designed in part to stimulate every student to study longer and harder. The policy was also a measure to compete with a nationwide chain of cram schools, Waseda Seminar, which was due to open a branch about 200 meters (666 feet) from Hoshino Seminar in April, 1998. The Waseda Seminar used another tactic, stressing the quality of its teaching.

It may be necessary for Japanese educators to reassess the current emphasis on preparing for examinations, which leads to so many children being enrolled in *juku*. Many students who attend both a regular school and cram school study from morning to late at night and are deprived of the free time and opportunities for play and other activities that are so necessary for their healthy development.

Parents and Children in Japanese Society

Many parents push their children to do well at school, and to concentrate on the goal of gaining admission to a good university. To improve their scholastic ability, children are sent to *juku*, or home tutors are hired, or both. A home tutor for a middle school student is paid about ¥2,000 ($16) or more per hour. Most parents can afford to pay the fees, but the more affluent spend more money on education; therefore the children of wealthy families are more successful, and tend to go to the more prestigious schools.

Children study day and night to live up to their parents' expectations; academic success becomes the most important object of their lives, and personal goals are sacrificed. This results in self-denial, which is related to Confucianism's filial duties. Children fulfil their filial duties by studying hard; those who do not sit at their desks for hours a day are seen as failing in their duties and may be punished by their parents. Consider the following extract from "Troubleshooter," the advice column of the daily *Yomiuri* (December 27, 1997):

Even 'elites' need to be nurtured

Q: I am a 37-year-old housewife. My husband and I have a son and a daughter and are well-off. However, my husband is extremely worrisome when it comes to his attitude toward our son's education. When our son, a first grader at an elementary school, neglects his studies, my husband shouts at him and sometimes gets violent. He threatens our son verbally and physically. Our son is always obedient, even when he is sobbing. He is tenacious but sensitive. He doesn't like sports. My husband is a member of a so-called elite. He believes that if one doesn't have a strong academic record, one's only option will be to work in a "dirty or miserable" job. He has our son believing this, too. I am worried that our son will become disheartened or violent. What should I do about the relationship between my husband and our son? Mrs. E, Tokyo

A: I wonder how your husband reconciles the fact that members of ultra-elites from big companies are being arrested one after another for violating the law under threats from sokaiya stock holders. A distinguished academic career doesn't assure future happiness. If a member of an elite, such as your husband, is someone who puts absolute value on school scores and uses violence, both verbal and physical, on his son without considering the boy's feelings, I don't want your son to be part of that elite. If your son, whom you describe as sensitive, continues to be abused physically and mentally, there is a possibility that his spirit will be broken, especially if sports are not an option for venting his frustration. Also, when he grows old enough to rebel against his father, he might use violence at home or become a delinquent. I think you should talk seriously with your husband about your concerns, and about the ill effects of putting so much emphasis on school grades. If he doesn't change, tell him that scolding alone will not encourage his son to study. Tell him that his son's scores will rise if he is allowed to take some joy in studying, such as in being praised for his efforts by his father. Also, try to arrange as many occasions as possible on which the family can have fun together. The bad influence your husband has had on his son may be lessened a little. Osaka University Professor

Not all men treat their sons so harshly, but one cannot overlook the reality that in Japan one's academic background determines, to a great extent, one's status and social position. Inevitably therefore, children are urged to study and to succeed academically: parents do not want their children to be considered failures. The advisor quoted above blames the husband, but the more fundamental problem is with the hierarchical nature of Japanese society itself. It is the society, not the husband, that "puts absolute value on school scores." Unless Japanese society itself changes, individual parents will continue to pressurize their children. Even if parents were to change their own behavior, the wider society would continue to emphasize academic achievement.

Parents' Attitudes towards the Five-day School Week

Many parents want their children to study at school six days a week. In March 1994 the Education Ministry conducted a survey of public attitudes, polling schoolchildren, teachers and parents for their views on the complete five-day school week, which would be implemented in the 2003 school year. Among parents, 47.2 % stated that "Saturday school holidays should not be increased," and 21.9 % said that it was "hard to say." The most common reasons for disapproval of a five-day school week were "some families cannot take care of children on Saturdays" (58.4%), "disruption of the children's life rhythm" (51.4%), "slower progress in school" (40.3%) and "children will simply spend more time playing" (35.2%).

Some parents, especially fathers, are actually so busy with their work on Saturdays that they have little time for taking care of their children; they expect schools to be responsible for all aspects of their children's lives, from "life rhythm" to studies, and they consider school discipline as a substitute for home training. Such dependency on school education stems from the view that one's profession is more essential than one's family life. As this view is dominant in Japan, it is not surprising that the six-day school week is preferred by parents (fathers), who make light of the significance of parent-child interaction and attach greater importance to their jobs.

It is possible that the new policy will increase parental involvement in education and decrease dependency on school education. The 30.9 % of parents in favor of schools being closed on Saturdays cited as reasons "a more relaxed life and more free time" (79.6%), "more time for family interaction" (67.0%), "more time to socialize (play) with friends" (40.5%) and "more time for activities involving contact with nature"(40.0%). On the other hand, there is no guarantee that the introduction of a five-day school week will actually reduce children's workload. The 1994 Education Ministry survey found that one reason for parents' disapproval of the five-day week was the possibility of a rise in attendance at private cram schools. Under the new system, more and more children would go to *juku* on Saturdays to learn techniques to pass entrance exams. Because the main problem is academic snobbism and the race for academic success, implementation of a five-day school week would not change the whole story.

High School Admission and Entrance Exams

Each year, about 97 % of middle school students are admitted to high schools. All applicants to high schools must take entrance exams, and these are usually held in early March for the school year beginning in April. Entrance exams for public high schools are administered by the prefectural or municipal board of education, which develops its own standardized exam based on the national curriculum. The exam is conducted simultaneously throughout each prefecture, and tests students on Japanese, mathematics, science, social studies and English. Most questions are multiple choice. Exam results are sent to the high schools to which students apply, and each school then conducts its own admissions process; the results are not released to the examinees. Private high schools create their own entrance exams. These cover from three to five subjects, and are held in January or February.

The selection criteria for public high school admission include exam results, *naishinsho* (student credentials) and other information. The *naishinsho* is an evaluation by the student's homeroom teacher of his or her academic and nonacademic performance. It usually consists of scholastic records (grades), records of special activities, behavior and personality records, attendance records, details of sports activities, cultural activities, social activities and volunteer activities. As with exam results, the *naishinsho* is not released to the students. Despite these various criteria for entrant selection, in most prefectures the emphasis is placed on the examination results. In famous private high schools, exam scores are even more crucial and little consideration is given to student credentials.

Emphasis on the results of entrance exams as an admission criterion influences students in their selection of schools to apply to. The homeroom teacher provides guidance to ensure that those who want to proceed to high school will be able to gain admission somewhere. Usually, a meeting is arranged for late fall or early winter, at which the homeroom teacher, the student and his or her parents discuss the student's grades and recent test scores, the parents' wishes and the teacher's recommendations. Students with lower grades or scores are advised not to apply to competitive high schools because failure is certain. The teacher's advice is almost always accepted.

Many students take the entrance exams of both competitive and non-competitive high schools, in case they fail to be admitted to the school of their choice. Famous high schools, of course, admit only the top middle school students.

High School Admission Reforms

The Education Ministry has been aware of the negative impact of entrance examination competition on the healthy development of students. In 1983, the "Committee to Improve Systems of Selecting Entrants to Upper Secondary Schools" was formed, and the following year the committee issued a report, "On Systems of Selecting Entrants to Upper Secondary Schools", on the basis of which, the ministry advised local boards of education to diversify selection methods and to employ multiple selection criteria including the extensive use of recommendation and interviews.

In April 1991 the Central Council for Education, an advisory panel to the Education Ministry, produced its own report, which also advocated further diversification of selection methods. Its perspective on the issue was as follows:

> The easing of entrance examination competition is vital to the reform of upper secondary education. This must be achieved through a variety of measures, including the use of diversified and multiple evaluation criteria in the selection process. It is vital to liberate students from the psychological pressure resulting from examination competition and the excessive emphasis on a standard score in order to create an education system that respects individuality and emphasizes humanity.

On the basis of these recommendations, the Education Ministry established an expert group, the "Committee on the Promotion of the Reform of Upper Secondary Education," to survey specific improvement measures. In February 1993, the ministry issued a notice, "On Systems of Selecting Entrants to Upper Secondary Schools."

Taking into account the advice from the Education Ministry, in fiscal 1994 seven prefectures reduced the number of subjects tested in entrance exams from five to three or four, and 23 prefectures administered weighted scoring on entrance exams. In some prefectures, schools are now permitted to prepare some of the exam questions, or students can select subject areas. In order to liberate students from the psychological pressure resulting from their having only one opportunity to take a public high school entrance exam in the same prefecture, five prefectures now allow candidates multiple opportunities to take entrance exams.

A number of prefectures have introduced admission based on recommendation, whereby a certain quota of applicants is admitted to a high school without taking an entrance exam. Instead student credentials, especially achievements in sports, cultural, social and various volunteer activities, are used as admission criteria. All the prefectures use interviews in one form or another. This method allows high schools to learn about applicants' personalities and attitudes, which are not evaluated through testing.

All of the above reforms apply to public high schools. Private high schools, despite encouragement from the Central Council for Education to diversify their selection procedures, still place priority on exam scores.

Reforms of Regular Exams in Higashi Middle School

It is not just high school entrance exams that place a psychological burden on students; all exams contribute to this effect. To reduce the stress on students, the principal of Higashi Middle School in Kanuma, Tochigi Prefecture, announced on February 23, 1998 the abolition of regular mid-term and end-of-term exams for the 1998 school year. School principals have discretion as to how to evaluate the scholastic progress of students.

According to the school principal, the existing exam-based grading system generates a number of problems. Students who get high scores are satisfied, but low-performing students are discouraged and their self-esteem is seriously damaged; as a result, they are prone to behave badly and get into trouble. The new method would focus on individual development based on the strong one-on-one relationship between teacher and student. Students would decide their study goals and workload in consultation with their teachers. Teachers would give students short tests during regular classes to check comprehension, and use interviews with students to assess their progress. Students would no longer take home report cards, as these are thought to discourage slow learners. This continuous assessment system is expected to help motivate students to study and to improve student life.

However a majority of parents are not in favor of the continuous assessment system. At a meeting in June 1997 to explain the new system to parents, some attendants questioned whether the measure would evaluate students accurately and improve their scholastic ability. Others doubted whether the system would help students pass a high school entrance exam. Some said that although children would be happy with continuous assessment, achieving success under the new method would not be easy as long as the current high school entrance exam remained in place. High schools to which Higashi Middle School students applied might not view their school records favorably, and if the new system did not work, it would be the students who suffered the most.

The mass media also criticized the school principal's decision, claiming that the abolition of examination competition in school would prevent students from being successful in market-oriented Japanese society, where one needs a competitive spirit to have a promising career. Certainly, the elimination of regular exams in one school will not change test-oriented education. In the current system, and under prevailing social attitudes, students will still have to study diligently at school and at home to perform well on entrance exams. They believe that their efforts are necessary for success in their future lives.

Test-oriented Japanese Education and "Standardized Children"

Testing is the key to Japanese education. It is the sole means of classifying students: this one should go to a prestigious high school, that one to a non-competitive school or vocational training center. It is no exaggeration to say that the result of an entrance exam determines the life opportunities of students. Thus, students are pressurized to study hard from a very early age, and while high-performing students are praised, poor learners are disregarded.

This all-or-nothing nature of testing does have some beneficial outcomes; for example, Japanese students do far better than their American counterparts in math and science. However placing too much emphasis on academic achievement may narrow the range of children's options and hinder the development of their talents. Each student has a different excellence (for example in music, arts, sports, foreign languages, etc.) that should be recognized and nurtured, not damaged by disproportionate emphasis on a one-size-fits-all testing approach.

Test-oriented Japanese education is made possible by the homogeneity and affluence of Japanese society; there are very few children from low-income, ethnic minority or transient families. Students in Japanese schools are regarded as "standardized children;" they are assumed to have the same potential and ability, and to be able therefore to learn the same material at the same rate. It is believed that study will ensure high test scores, and low achievers are blamed for their lack of effort.

Such a system could not be adopted in the multiracial and multicultural context of the United States, where many children belong to low-income families and may be too hungry to concentrate on lessons. This difference in the social context between Japan and the United States leads to different concepts of testing. In Japan, testing classifies students, while in the United States, test results are used more as a means to tell how children are doing in school. In American schools, testing does not classify as failures children who may only reach their full potential later in life.

Environmental Education

The test-centered system in Japanese schools has ignored environmental education, resulting in a total lack of environmental awareness. This is reflected in people's lifestyles, which feature over-packaged consumer goods and a preference for buying new items rather than repairing old ones. Parked cars are left with engines running, with no thought to the waste or pollution involved. Environmental protection is given very low priority.

Recently, however, the Education Ministry has been making an effort to instill environmental awareness in children, to help them respect nature and protect and improve the environment.

Since fiscal 1990, the ministry has been implementing the following measures:

- Preparation and distribution of teachers' reference materials and case studies for elementary schools
- Preparation and distribution of materials for middle and high schools
- Designation of model municipalities for promotion of environmental education (10 municipalities)
- Implementation of Environmental Education Fairs (fiscal 1994 onward)
- Seminars for teachers in charge of environmental education (fiscal 1994 onward)

Whether or not these measures are effective is not the point. The fact remains that the Education Ministry always has to take the initiative on major educational reforms, including the issue of the environment, while local school officials simply wait for instructions. In the same way, the general public looks to the government for leadership on environmental problems. For this reason, grass-roots environmental movements are almost nonexistent in Japan. Unless people are inspired to think independently, environmental education may have short-term effects, but will be ineffective in the long run.

Extracurricular School Excursions

Japanese schools offer a number of extracurricular activities, which are intended to enhance the experience of school and encourage otherwise reluctant students to attend regularly. Athletic meetings are held several times a year, and there are cultural, music and other festivals. A proper combination of studies and extracurricular activities in middle school education has so far had positive results.

The most popular extracurricular activities for middle school students are school trips, when students and their teachers travel by bus or train to a lake, mountain, or national park, or to a museum or historical shrine. The trips are mandatory, and school uniform must be worn. Students also go on camping trips, and in the third year of middle school, they go on a week-long school excursion to a location chosen by teachers. Those who live in the country usually go to a big city; city-dwellers go to the countryside. When I was at middle school I went to Kyoto, the former capital of Japan, and Osaka, the second biggest city. We traveled by *Shinkansen*, bullet train, which runs at a speed of about 160 mph. In Kyoto, students visited several famous Shinto shrines built well over 1,000 years ago, and in Osaka we entered the beautiful Osaka

113

castle. We stayed at a reasonable hotel, and at dinnertime, many of us ate as much food as we could - second helpings were free!

Elementary and high school students also go on relatively long school trips. When I was a sixth grader, I went to Tokyo for four days. Students visited the Japanese Diet and the famous Tokyo Tower; we stayed in a lodge and, of course, boys ate as much food as they could! As a second year student in high school, I went on a week-long school excursion to Chugoku, west of Osaka, where we visited a number of famous historical places and national parks. This trip was less enjoyable, because of the teachers' choice of sites to visit. From their viewpoint, a school trip is an opportunity for social studies; visiting historical museums, shrines or the Japanese Diet helps broaden students' knowledge and increase their social experience. Students, however, want to enjoy themselves.

Extracurricular Club Activities

Most students take part in optional extracurricular clubs after regular classes. They can choose between sports clubs (baseball, softball, volleyball, rugby, soccer, tennis, table tennis, track, badminton, judo, kendo or swordsmanship, swimming, dance, etc) and culture clubs (English, broadcasting, debating, science, mathematics, computer, music, Japanese chess, calligraphy, ceramic art, etc). These club activities play an important educational role in the healthy mental and physical development of students, and recognizing this, the Education Ministry is implementing practical research for the promotion of club activities. It also helps to provide schools with club instructors or instructor training programs.

The school approves the establishment of clubs, and they are managed by teachers, who also act as club instructors. Teachers in charge of club activities are busy: they spend several hours a week on club management in addition to instructing regular classes. According to a survey conducted by the Tochigi Teaching Personnel Conference in Tochigi Prefecture in October 1997, more than half the teachers in charge of club activities felt club instruction was a burden on them or expressed a desire to be free of it. The survey, which was part of the research on the five-day school week, polled 1,757 elementary school teachers (83.6 % responded) and 558 middle school teachers (65.6 % responded). It found that 94.8 % of elementary schools ran extracurricular clubs, which were supervised by 56 % of teachers. In middle schools, almost all the teachers (93.9 %) managed club activities nearly everyday; 51.9 % of them directed 20-25 days a month and 37.3 % more than 25 days; on a weekly basis, 36.6 % instructed 5-9 hours. Asked if club instruction was a burden on them, 45.4 % of elementary school teachers and 48 % of middle school teachers said that they "can not help but continue to direct clubs albeit a burden;" 23.9 % and 12 % said that they "want to quit if possible" and 20.7 % and 34.5 % said that they were content with it although they were busy. About 90 % of elementary and middle school teachers suggested the separation of teaching duties from responsibility for directing club activities. If club instructors were selected from the wider community, teachers would have more time for textbook research.

Sports clubs meet for approximately two hours from 3:30 to 5:30 P.M. each day after regular classes; some students continue to practice as late as 9:00 P.M. Some sports clubs continue to meet at weekends and during school vacations. Culture club activities are held two or three times a week. More students become involved in clubs in rural areas, since in the cities students are more likely to attend *juku* and spend their time preparing for competitive exams. In summer third-year students quit clubs to prepare for high school entrance exams.

When new students join a club, the senior students welcome them, give an orientation and train them in a manner similar to their own teachers' manner of disciplining students. Newcomers are supposed to serve upperclassmen and do odd jobs, especially in male sports clubs. In a tennis club, for example, first-year students are expected to chase tennis balls for their elders, and are allowed to use the courts only while the upperclassmen take a break or when they have finished practicing. After the club activity, the new students put the courts in order, and may be required to buy food or soft drinks for the senior students. If such an order is ignored, they are severely scolded or may be physically punished. When I joined a school table tennis club, I spent a year collecting balls, and often went to a nearby shop to buy chocolate, chewing gum, cans of Coke and the like for the third-year students. Newcomers learn the pecking order of the club by obeying and observing the upperclassmen. Those who cannot endure the club discipline quit, but most survive the training in the hope of becoming upperclassmen themselves after a year. This is a ruler-ruled relationship similar in function to the teacher-student relationship.

Sports club members have opportunities to participate in the National Middle School Athletic Meet (17 sports) and the National High School General Athletic Meet (30 sports). The Education Ministry provides prefectures with subsidies to pay for organization and transportation for these events. The school provides support for club activities and encourages students to practice hard to win competitions. If a sports club is successful in a

117

prefectural competition or tournament, its members get prizes and honor, and the team qualifies for the national competition. Success in the national championship wins prestige for the school, which might then attract able students for admission in the next school year. Culture clubs too have opportunities to shine: their activities are demonstrated at culture or music festivals.

Despite the discipline involved, students enjoy club activities, which provide them with peer group socialization. Within the clubs children can cultivate friendships and solidify group spirit by sharing joy and sorrow. Indeed, it is this aspect of school life that children tend to find most enjoyable. According to a survey by the Education Ministry in March 1994, 70.6 % of middle school students and 64 % of high school students were satisfied or fairly satisfied with school life. Middle school students were pleased with "playing and socializing with friends" (93.9 %), "club and extracurricular club activities" (50.8 %) and "school events" (42.0 %). For high school students, "playing and socializing with friends" (92.5 %) came first, followed by "school events"(40.1%) and "club and extracurricular club activities" (39.8%). Moreover, this early establishment of strong peer group ties prepares children for later: such ties, less flatteringly known as "cronyism," are important throughout Japanese society, in business, politics and other social dealings.

Surveys on Students' After School Activities

In October 1997 the Tochigi Comprehensive Education Center in Tochigi Prefecture conducted a survey on children's after school activities; it polled 2,400 second, fifth, eighth, and eleventh graders (600 each) and received 2,324 responses. The survey, released on May 20, 1998, found that while nearly 90 % of second graders usually or sometimes played with friends after school, 54.7 % of eighth grade boys and 71.8 % of eighth grade girls hardly ever played. More than 90 % of fifth graders studied at home, but 57.9 % of eleventh graders rarely sat at their desks. When having difficulties with schoolwork, elementary students usually asked for help from their mothers, while middle school students relied on friends, followed by mothers, cram school teachers, siblings and schoolteachers; high school students would usually consult friends or schoolteachers. Asked how much free time they had after school, 43.8 % of elementary students, 58.6 % of middle school students and 68.5 % of high school students said three hours. Asked how many books they read a week, 26.8 % of second graders said "a few", but 24.8 % of second graders, 34.1 % of fifth graders, 65.5 % of eighth graders and 80.4 % of eleventh graders said they hardly read. Among fifth graders, 21.5 % said they seldom read newspapers; the figure for eighth graders was 25.6 %, and for eleventh graders 27.4 %. Many more children reported watching TV more than two hours a day: 29.3 % of second graders, 59.5 % of fifth graders, 72.5 % of eighth graders and 68.1 % of eleventh graders. As for bedtime, 66.1 % of second graders went to bed by 9:00 P.M., 52 % of fifth graders at 10:00 P.M., 53.3 % of eighth graders at 11:00 P.M. and 47.7 % of eleventh graders at midnight. Around 30 % of students get up by themselves in the morning, and one in four high school students is woken up by others. Analyzing these results, the center concluded that children spend most of their free time watching TV, and that they are not very interested in reading books or newspapers.

Improving Students' Reading Skills

Teachers are aware of the lack of reading skills among students. Many schools now have a morning reading hour, to get students used to reading. Research conducted by book distributor Tohan Corp. found that 369 schools held morning reading hours in the 1998 school year, up more than 100 from the previous year. The survey also found that books help to improve students' behavior. In more than 80 % of schools holding the reading sessions, teachers acknowledged a difference in students' attitudes, presumably because quiet time reading helps children to understand other people's emotions and feelings, and to act accordingly.

The reading hour does not impose texts on children. Students who cannot concentrate on academic books are allowed to bring books of their choice, and for those new to reading, boards of education provide easy-to-read books. The four basic principles of a successful reading hour are that all the students in the reading sessions participate; there is reading on all weekdays for consistency; students make their own choice of books, in order to develop individuality; and there are no assignments - just reading.

The reading hour is perhaps more efficient than free study periods, in which students are supposed to complete study sheets, but are often so bored that they talk to each other, play games or disturb other students.

A Survey on Students' Sense of Values

A survey by the Tokyo Metropolitan Government polled fifth and eighth graders (1,760 responded) on children's happiness and the worries in their lives. The results, released in May 1998, revealed that 94.3 % of elementary students enjoyed playing with their friends and 51.7 % were satisfied with school events. Among middle school students, 91 % enjoyed playing with their friends and

41.7 % were content with extracurricular club activities. Asked what they did not like about school, 49 % of fifth graders said "nothing particular," and 45.7 % of eighth graders said, "Studies are not interesting." Asked to whom they talk about their day to day worries, 22.7 % of fifth graders and 17.5 % of eighth graders said they relied on schoolteachers, and 7.7 % of fifth graders and 20.5 % of eighth graders sought advice from private cram school teachers. Nearly 90 % of eighth graders usually or sometimes felt exhausted; around 40 % thought that "money is the most important thing" and 26.9 % felt that they wanted to destroy things. Asked to what extent their parents understand them, children said that 96 % of mothers and 84.7 % of fathers knew their school records, and 91.2 % of mothers and 76.2 % of fathers were aware of their habits or traits. About 80 % of mothers and about 40 % of fathers know their children's friends and acquaintances, and how they spend money. Only 42.6 % of mothers and 24.2 % of fathers recognize their children's anxieties; and 51.7 % of mothers and 38.7 % of fathers know their children's ambitions. The Tokyo Metropolitan Government concluded that children do not have many reliable adults to talk to about their worries, and that they are materialistic.

The Paradox of Freedom in American and Japanese Education

While their American counterparts define their own values and challenge the authority of teachers and parents, Japanese students absorb a set of absolute values - all should study, learn, and obey teachers. While Americans love freedom and independence, and fight against oppressive government and law, in Japan civil disobedience is an alien concept. Japanese children typically obey their parents and teachers without question, just as the Japanese people accept judgements by the authorities and laws enacted by the legislature. The government is considered beneficial to the people, who do not have to resist to protect their human rights. Far from feeling deprived of their liberty by the authorities, the Japanese enjoy freedom "provided" by the government.

Although adult Americans largely use peaceful means of civil disobedience, such as demonstrations and sit-down tactics, an increasing number of youngsters tend to resort to lethal means to find an outlet for their rage and frustrations. Parents and teachers should perhaps teach the notion of passive resistance so that children assert themselves calmly, staging a sit-in, for example, instead of committing serious crimes incompatible with democracy. Excessive freedom and easy access to firearms cause school problems far more serious than those in Japan. According to a study by the U.S Education Department released in mid-March 1998, about 10 % of public schools in America experienced serious school violence in the 1996-97 school year, including armed assaults and rape. 6,039 students - 56 % of whom were high school students, 34 % middle school students and 9 % grade school students - were expelled from school in 1996-97. Fifty-eight percent of these were dismissed for bringing handguns to school and referred to the police.

However, it is impossible to prevent guns entering school. About half of American households have guns. In a 1993 national survey of sixth- to twelfth-graders, 15 % said that they had carried a gun in the previous month, and 4 % said that they had brought a gun to school in the previous year. A survey by the Center for Disease Control and Prevention (CDC) also found that in 1995, about 1 in 12 students carried a firearm. Therefore, a combination of youngsters' immaturity and the easy availability of firearms makes fatal school shootings inevitable. On December 1, 1997, a 14-year-old student at Heath High School in West Paducah, Ky, killed three girls with semiautomatic handgun. On March 24, 1998, two boys aged 11 and 13, armed with rifles and pistols and dressed in camouflage shirts and hats, killed four girls and a teacher. On April 24, 1998, a pupil at Parker Middle School in Edinborg, Pa murdered a teacher at a school graduation dance. On May 21, 1998, a 15-year-old boy killed his parents at home and then two students of the Thurston High School in Springfield, Ore.

The first comprehensive survey of gun-related deaths - murders, suicides and accidents - published in the *International Journal of Epidemiology* (April, 1998), found that in 1994, of the world's 36 richest nations, the United States had the highest rate of gun deaths, at 14.24 per 100,000 people; and that Japan had the lowest rate, at 0.05 per 100,000. The United States accounted for 45 % of the 88,649 gun deaths reported, while in Japan there were only 124 gun-related deaths that year. Among other countries with low rates were South Korea, Hong Kong, Mauritius, Singapore, and Taiwan. This suggests a connection between the Asian system and social stability.

In Japan, its Firearms and Swords Control Law tightly controls the purchase, possession, and use of firearms; as a result, shooting crime cases totaled only 148 in 1996, according to a National Police Agency survey released on January 26, 1998. Of these, 124 were related to crime syndicate disputes or gangsters who illegally possess handguns, semiautomatic guns or other firearms. There were no school shootings reported.

If the purchase, possession and use of firearms were made illegal with only a few exceptions in the United States, as they are in Japan, shooting cases in American schools would be substantially decreased. It is pointless to say that the National Rifle Association is so powerful that the government cannot take effective measures against possessing arms. There are many problems inherent in American liberalism, which permits a culture of violence. American culture tolerates people resolving disputes and expressing anger and passion with weapons, and this romance with violence has been maintained under a tradition of a free government. American liberalism and the culture of violence are inseparable, the result being that government cannot severely limit the availability of guns, without impinging on the freedom that is fundamental to American society.

It would be wrong, however, to suggest that Japanese schools do not have their own problems. Strict discipline is no panacea. As the following sections will show, schools in Japan have been fighting their own battles, against truancy, violence, and juvenile delinquency; and the most vulnerable members of the school community - the disabled, the less academically gifted, and those experiencing stress and psychological problems, are not well served by the current school system.

Disabled Students

Disabled people tend to be looked down upon in Japanese society, and are considered inferior to their able-bodied peers. At school, students who are disabled or at all "different" are laughed at and humiliated. It is not surprising then that disabled students are discouraged from attending regular schools.

Teachers are opposed to having disabled students studying in ordinary classes. Mildly disabled students are entitled to attend regular schools, but find that school principals are reluctant to admit them, fearing that they might hinder lessons or disturb other students in the classroom. The school may claim that it does not have appropriate facilities, when in fact it simply does not want to take on the responsibility of caring for such special needs. Teachers are reluctant to give the extra attention necessary to disabled children, believing that carrying out the national curriculum has priority over special education.

There have been some advances. Modern technology enables disabled children to live much fuller lives: there are buses equipped with lifts and ramps for wheelchairs, lights at pedestrian crossings with accompanying tunes for the visually impaired, and toilets for the disabled in public facilities. Even so, disabled children are unwilling to go out, because they are afraid of being mocked; they become depressed and reluctant to participate in social activities. They need an unbiased society in which they can express themselves comfortably and fulfil their potential. In the rigid social hierarchy in Japan, that seems a very long way off.

Truancy

According to annual surveys carried out by the Education Ministry, in fiscal 1996 19,500 elementary students (one in every 415.9 pupils) and 74,800 middle school students (one in every 60.6) were truant from school at least 30 days, an increase on the previous year of around 2,900 elementary students and 9,700 middle school students. This was the fifth consecutive year in which figures had risen. Reasons for cutting classes were problems with other students or bullying (19.7%), poor school records (13.2%) and family problems, including domestic violence, divorce and poverty (9.5%).

Education analysts attribute the increase in truancy in part to lax graduation requirements in middle school. Unlike high schools, middle schools do not require regular attendance and satisfactory examination results for students to graduate. If a school deems that low-performing or low-attendance students have made "an effort to study," they are awarded graduation certificates.

A survey conducted by the Tokyo Metropolitan Government in November 1997 showed a link between truancy and home violence. The government polled 4,500 men and women in Tokyo, of whom 1,226 men and 1,553 women responded. Fifty-two women abused by their male companions were also interviewed. More than half of the women interviewed said that their partners also abused their children, either physically or psychologically, or both. Most of the respondents believed that their children refused to attend school because they were so upset by the violence at home. The survey found that one out of every three children who was the victim of violence, and one out of every five children who knew of the father's violent behavior toward the mother, did not go to school.

The Education Ministry is stepping up efforts to reduce truancy by commissioning prefectures and municipalities to implement adaptation assistance programs. Truant students are given opportunities to undergo individual counseling, participate in group activities and receive instruction in various subjects in education centers or other facilities. In fiscal 1994 such programs were administered by 82 organizations, up 11 from the previous year. Other measures include the provision of in-service teacher training, the preparation and distribution of teachers' reference materials, and the operation of model programs to improve educational counseling. In fiscal 1997, the Education Ministry provided financial support for seven municipalities in Tokyo, Fukuoka, Gifu and Wakayama prefectures to use e-mail to communicate with truant students. Some teachers even used videoconferencing facilities to teach truant students who had problems interacting with others. Results have so far been positive, and the ministry plans to promote this approach for as long as it is successful.

Some private cram schools offer truant students services similar to projects supported by the Education Ministry. In April 1998 a cram school in Misato, Saitama Prefecture, began correspondence courses using e-mail and fax. Two courses with 30 minutes of daily work cost ¥50,000 ($400) per term (four terms a year). The school said that its programs would save children who would otherwise be left behind by the current education system. Nevertheless, education analysts still claim that education based on face-to-face interaction between teacher and student is preferable to e-mail-based education.

Violation of School Rules

Despite strict school discipline, a minority of students violate regulations in order to ease or release the stress caused by so many rules and the pressure to achieve academically. Low-performing students in particular tend to smoke, drink or use stimulant drugs. Some male students read obscene magazines or use telephone club dating services. Some girls engage in *enjo kosai* (compensated dating), a form of prostitution.

A 1997 survey by a national conference of parent-teacher associations polled 2,400 sets of parents and children across the country. The survey found that one out of every five children shoplifted or smoked, one in seven called telephone clubs, one out of every 60 had tried illegal drugs and one out of every 170 had experienced *enjo kosai.* The survey also found that 90 % of parents believed that their third-year middle school children never engaged in these prohibited acts. Parents pointed out that television has a negative influence on children's behavior.

The tendency of below-average students to violate school rules is related to the teaching philosophy that "all students can learn." Lower ability students may not be able to achieve satisfactory test scores even if they study long and hard, yet the teacher attributes their poor scores to lack of effort and tells them to study more: as a result, they become enraged. Moreover, the homeroom teacher, who is busy preparing promising students to pass competitive high school entrance exams, does not have time to help those with failing marks. Ignored by teachers or simply feeling bored and frustrated at school, low-performing students turn to wrongdoing, including school violence.

School Violence

According to a report released by the Education Ministry on December 22, 1997, school violence is on the rise. In fiscal 1996, violence against teachers and school facilities, violence among students and cases of bullying in schools totaled 10,575, up 31.7 % from the previous year, and the highest number since the first survey conducted in 1983. The problem was at its worst in middle schools, where violent acts totaled 8,169, a 37.2 % increase on the previous year.

The increase in school violence is mirrored by the general escalation in juvenile crime. A report released by the National Police Agency on December 18, 1997 revealed that from January to November in 1997, 139,867 teenagers (14.7 minors out of every 1,000) were placed in police custody on suspicion of criminal offenses, the highest figures since 1988. Of those arrested, 2,085 had committed serious crimes. There were 5,910 arrests on suspicion of threatening behavior, an increase of 13.7 % on the previous year. A record number of 1,535 minors including 181 middle school students were arrested on suspicion of robbery-related offenses, a 58 % increase. There were fewer arrests for murder however: 70 compared with 82 the previous year. Regarding the abuse of stimulant drugs, 1,509 minors including 249 middle and high school students were held by police, a 12 % rise.

In the Osaka Prefecture, violence against teachers in middle schools rose significantly in 1997. At one school, four third-year students were arrested in the middle of December 1997 on suspicion of assaulting a teacher and smashing school windows. At the end of October that year, a 45-year-old male teacher had witnessed the four boys grabbing a tennis racket from a younger student. When he intervened, he was beaten by the four students, one of whom fell to the ground with the teacher in the struggle. After the attack, one of the suspects took a photograph of the teacher as he lay injured. Meanwhile, the four boys became enraged when the school principal prohibited them from riding their motorcycles, one of which had been stolen, on school premises. On November 20, they retaliated by breaking two windows in the principal's office with an iron bar. After the arrest of the four suspects, the prefectural police sent specialists in juvenile delinquency to middle schools across the prefecture to warn students and to advise teachers on how to handle violent students.

In Washimiya, Saitame Prefecture, a 15-year-old male student was arrested on March 2, 1998 on suspicion of assaulting a teacher. The third-year student at a public junior school hit a 42-year-old teacher in the abdomen and hip after the teacher demanded he remove his earrings while in school. In the same month, a 15-year-old male student at a middle school in Seta, Gunma Prefecture, repeatedly kicked a female teacher after she told him not to bring his mobile phone to school. The same teacher had been kicked in the shoulder by another male student in February. In this case, the teacher talked to the school principal and other teachers and decided to inform the police. The principal was at first unwilling to report the case, but did so because not reporting it would ultimately not benefit the student, and because he wanted to teach the students that they would be arrested if they committed violent acts.

In an extreme case, again in March 1998, police arrested four middle school students on suspicion of violence at the Ashikaga Municipal Yamabe Middle School in Ashikaga, Tochigi Prefecture. The four boys, all 14-year-old second-year students, had kicked and beaten seven teachers and three fellow students. Early in March they had been found wandering the school building while classes were in session, carrying bats and metal pipes. A teacher who challenged the boys was beaten-up. On March 18, the boys smashed school windows using bats and metal pipes, and they threw rocks at other windows, breaking eight windows in all.

School officials said later that one of the suspects hardly ever went to school and another tended to cut classes. The four boys told the police that they committed this violence to vent pent-up frustrations.

Bullying

The most serious problem in Japanese schools and the most significant cause of truancy is bullying - the psychological or physical abuse of students by peers. This is predominantly a male activity but girls are occasionally involved. Perpetrators threaten timid, small or vulnerable students in a closed room or on an empty street corner, often demanding money. If money is not given, the weak are beaten up. Unless serious injury results, the cases are covered up or overlooked because most victims fear retaliation and so do not relate the incidents to teachers or parents. Nevertheless, 21,733 cases of bullying in elementary schools were recorded by the Education Ministry in 1997; in middle schools, 25,862; and in high schools, 3,771.

A survey released by the Management and Coordination Agency in April 1998 revealed that a third of elementary and middle school students had been bullied by peers. The survey on bullying, school violence and absenteeism polled 58 public elementary schools and 107 public middle schools in Tokyo and 17 prefectures in October and November 1997, and 16,824 students, 15,714 parents and 785 teachers responded. The results of the survey show that most teachers and parents do not realize the true extent of the problem and fail to take effective measures. Many cases remain unresolved, and the victims continue to suffer.

30.4 % of students actually admitted that they had bullied peers. The survey found that 4.1 % of students (5.3% of elementary students and 3.5% of middle school students) "are currently being bullied," and 33.1 % of students (36.4% of elementary students and 31.4% of middle school students) "have experienced bullying". Only 15 % of parents knew that "their children suffer bullying." Of the bullied students, 39.4% told their parents, 37.8 % "endured the sufferings without consulting anyone," 30.1 % resisted the bullies and 29.0 % consulted teachers. 27.4% of students (36.5% of elementary students and 22.7% of middle school students) "have been attacked by their peers at school" over the past year, but only 4.6% of their parents said that they knew. Of the 55.4 % of children who had seen someone being bullied, 28.1 % of elementary students and 52.4% of middle school students "did nothing". 30.5% of students said that their parents did not advise them on how to cope with such a situation. 19.3 % of all students said that they had skipped school several or many times, because of bullying and other problems at school.

All the teachers polled stated that they took measures to deal with school violence: 96% said that they had intervened to prevent bullying, and 80% had talked with the parents of bullied children; however 14 % of the victims and 19.3 % of their parents said that teachers did nothing to contain bullying.   44.1% of teachers admitted that early detection of school violence and bullying was difficult, and 43.1 % complained that they could not get help from parents.

In extreme cases, victims are driven to commit suicide to escape the bullying. On March 20, 1998, a 14-year-old student at Toyama Middle School in Narita, Chiba Prefecture, hanged himself in the storage room of his house, leaving a note saying that he had paid ¥80,000 ($640) to a 17-year-old boy, but he could not pay the remaining ¥40,000 ($320), and that he preferred to die rather than be beaten up. The 17-year-old had graduated from Toyama Middle School two years previously and had begun high school, but had dropped out and was then unemployed. He had begun bullying about a year before, and in September 1997 he extorted ¥30,000 ($240) from another student. Teachers knew of the incident and warned the extortionist, who later attacked the 14-year-old boy, believing that he had told school officials about the incident. In early March 1998, he demanded ¥40,000 from the 14-year-old, who refused and was punched and had a lighted cigarette pressed into his right hand, causing wounds that needed 10 days to heal. Five days after his second victim's suicide, the assailant was arrested on suspicion of forcibly demanding money.

On April 9, 1998, another 17-year-old, a third-year-student at the private Wakamatsu Daiichi High School high school, was found dead at his home in the Fukushima Prefecture. He had hanged himself. The student had talked to his father and homeroom teacher about being bullied, and had expressed his wish to quit school. The teacher had visited his home on April 1 and 6.

In 1996 and 1997 the Tokyo Metropolitan Government's Institute for Educational Research carried out research at a kindergarten, two elementary schools and two middle schools. A total of about 5,200 children completed a questionnaire, and 2,000 of them were interviewed. This was the first large-scale survey to analyze the psychology of bullies, and might help educators detect bulling.

The motives for bullying were found to be hatred, revenge, control of others, malicious enjoyment, seeking an outlet for anger and frustration, or having victims take the blame for infringements of school rules. The survey revealed that kindergarten children often released their stress in the form of violence, and that they were prone to tease others out of uncontrolled frustration. Elementary students tended to form a group of friends and bully quiet or isolated students who behaved differently or ignored orders from the group. The victims were sometimes forced to play the role of the accused in a fake trial and were humiliated or compelled to wrestle with bigger students. Teachers were usually unaware of the incidents.

It was also found that teachers often believed the cunning, assertive and influential aggressors and blamed passive and quiet victims who were afraid of revealing details of the incidents. To resolve bullying problems, the study concluded that teachers should listen fairly to both parties, and that they should tell the perpetrators that any justification of bullying is wrong.

The remorseless hierarchy of the school encourages bullying by developing the notion that justice is the will of the strong. The weak must obey the strong or pain is inflicted on them. The strong do not regard the weak as equals, and so abuse their human rights. The study found that the older students are, the more they think the responsibility for bullying rests with the victims. Many middle school students tended to tolerate bullying: although 48.6% said, "bullying cannot be allowed, no matter what," 40.9% of third-year students said, "they take a wait-and-see attitude toward bullying." The students' toleration of bullying reflects the attitude of teachers toward corporal punishment. The teacher surreptitiously inflicts pain on students who break school rules; bullies, imitating the teachers' violence, abuse peers who do not listen to them or do not give them money. Therefore, unless teachers stop corporal punishment, students will not think that bullying is wrong.

The courts do not seem sensitive to the problems of bulling, which suggests that Japanese society tolerates bullying and does not fully respect human rights. The amount of compensatory damages paid in cases of bullying is small. On October 29, 1997, the Nagoya High Court ordered that a local government and 13 parents of seven former elementary students pay damages for a bullying case that had occurred six years earlier. The plaintiff, who was now 17, had been wounded in an attack by a group of his classmates when he was a fifth grader in September 1991. Because of this, he had been absent from school for about six months, and he was continuously harassed even after his return to school. The defendants claimed that there had been no bullying, and did not apologize to the victim. The plaintiff had demanded ¥3.2 million ($26,600) in damages, but in November 1996 the low court had awarded only ¥350,000 ($3,000); he appealed on the grounds that the damages awarded would not act as a deterrent to other bullies, and the high court increased the award to ¥600,000 ($5,000).

Knife-Wielding Teenagers

In early 1998, crimes committed by teenagers using knives suddenly became the center of public attention. On January 28, a 13-year-old male student stabbed a female teacher to death with a butterfly knife. The boy, a first-year student at the municipal Kuroiso Kita Middle School in Kuroiso, Tochigi Prefecture, stabbed his 26-year-old English teacher seven times in a school hallway after she reprimanded him for arriving late to class. The culprit is said to have been an ordinary, low profile student, whose sudden change of behavior shocked the nation. Some education analysts argued that his crime was a protest against severe and strictly enforced school rules, and a sign that the education system or the wider community is not functioning well. The boy is now held at a juvenile center, since under the Juvenile Law, those who are 14 or younger are not subject to criminal proceedings.

On February 2, 1998, in Tokyo's Koto Ward, a 15-year-old male middle school student used a knife to assault a bicycle patrolman in an attempt to steal his pistol. The officer was wearing protective clothing and was not harmed by the knife, but he did receive minor injuries to his head during the ensuing struggle. The student was arrested on suspicion of attempted robbery-murder and violation of the Firearms and Swords Control Law, which forbids the carrying of knives with blades measuring more than six centimeters (about two and a half inches). He told the police that he had the urge to shoot a real gun and had decided to get one by attacking a police officer.

On March 9, 1998, in Higashi Matsuyama, Saitama Prefecture, a 13-year-old middle school boy stabbed a schoolmate to death. The boy had been quarreling with several other students during a morning break, when he took out a knife and stabbed one of them. The assailant was arrested on suspicion of assault resulting in death. The boy was said to be a troublemaker, and he and the victim had been on bad terms. After the incident, the school principal held an emergency meeting and appealed for calm. He claimed that the school had taught students to respect human life, but had not checked whether students carried weapons.

On March 10, 1998, the National Police Agency released a study on 31 reported juvenile knife crimes perpetrated between January and mid-February. In 21 cases, minors committed crimes with malicious intent, and 17 of them could not control their criminal impulses. In the remaining 10 cases, offenders had quarreled with or been reprimanded by teachers or acquaintances before the incidents, and had been driven by anger over minor altercations rather than by any premeditation to commit a crime using a knife; they had carried knives initially for self-defense. Middle school and high school students were involved in 12 and 11 of 31 incidents, respectively. Kitchen knives were used in five cases, butterfly knives in 12 cases, and pocketknives in 14 cases. Most of the offenders had records of delinquency.

Prevention of Juvenile Knife Crimes

On February 3, 1998, following a spate of juvenile crimes involving knives, the government urged local school officials to inspect students' belongings brought to school. Prime Minister Ryutaro Hashimoto also instructed each Cabinet minister to map out measures to stop juvenile knife crimes. Education Minister Nobutaka Machimura held an emergency meeting in Tokyo with officials in the fields of student counseling and social education from all 47 prefectures and 12 major cities. Juvenile crime division officers from the National Police Agency also attended. Machimura told educators that inspections of students' bags should be allowed with the principal's permission, and that principals should explain to students and parents why such searches were necessary. School officials were advised to teach students the illegality of bringing knives and other dangerous objects to school and to educate them on the value of human life. On March 10, Machimura made a speech calling on children to stop carrying and committing crimes with knives.

On February 7, 1998, the Management and Coordination Agency said that it would distribute cards giving information on counseling services to the nation's 4.5 million middle school students. The cards, intended to reduce school violence and bullying, would be distributed to students before the summer vacation. Many students were not familiar with the services provided by counseling facilities set up by local governments and the police, and it was hoped that by accessing these, they might be able to solve their problems without recourse to violence.

On March 6, 1998, Prime Minister Hashimoto addressed the first meeting of a panel aiming at the prevention of juvenile crime. He said, "The problems that children face at school and home are serious. If we ignore the problems, our country will suffer in the future. The problems will not be solved by isolated measures, nor will educational reforms alone settle them. The crux of the issue is what kind of society we should have." The panel would discuss teenagers' actions and attitudes and their social and home environments, and then present recommendations to the government on how to reduce youth crime. The panel was made up of the Prime Minister, the Education Minister, the Chief Cabinet Secretary, the Chairman of the National Public Safety Commission, the heads of government advisory bodies on education and youth, psychiatric and television industry experts, and a cartoonist.

On March 16, 1998, the Tokyo Metropolitan Middle School Association held a meeting to authorize inspections of students' bags, and to come up with measures to encourage cooperation with police. On the question of searches, however, educators across the country were divided: many argued that inspections of students' bags might violate the right to privacy. In accordance with instructions from their prefectural boards of education, some schools carried out anonymous searches of students' belongings, but many schools did not carry out any inspections, fearing that such searches would undermine the trust between teacher and student.

For their part, local governments considered a prohibition on the sale of knives (especially butterfly knives) to those younger than 18. By early February no fewer than 29 prefectural governments had begun revising the ordinances concerning these harmful playthings. A National Police Agency survey released on April 30, 1998 showed that 36 prefectural governments had amended their ordinances to prohibit selling butterfly knives to minors.

According to a survey by the *Yomiuri Shimbun* newspaper, a majority of people agreed with regulations controlling the sale of knives to minors. The survey polled 3,000 people on February 21-22: 1,984 responded, of whom 85 % said they were tolerant of restrictions on selling edged implements to minors, and 81% agreed that teachers should inspect students' belongings. Seventy-six percent were in favor of revisions to the Juvenile Law to impose criminal penalties on children younger than 16 years old.

On March 24, 1998, the Education Ministry released a report recommending that school officials strengthen cooperation with the police and counseling institutions to deter high-profile student delinquency. The report, compiled by an advisory panel to the ministry, stressed that educators could not be expected to resolve all problems involving student discipline, and suggested that teachers seek assistance from appropriate agencies in order to deal with difficult situations. It also advised schools to form study groups to exchange information with the police and child counseling centers.

The report pointed out that before committing serious crimes, juvenile delinquents are apt to show signs of maladjustment, for example, mental or physical illness, or overreaction to trivial matters. In two of the murder cases in early 1998, the offenders were both first-year middle school students who had been disruptive and unmanageable at their elementary schools. The report recommended that elementary schools appoint special counseling teachers to provide children with adequate supervision and guidance, and it urged elementary and middle schools to exchange information and to cooperate in coordinating the guidance offered to students. Teachers should be encouraged to share information about individual delinquent cases with all the teaching staff, and should punish disruptive or violent students heavily but by non-corporal means, for instance, by suspension from school or by making students pay for the damage they cause. Such punishment would not undermine the relationship of trust between teacher and student.

On April 29, 1998, a government council on juvenile problems submitted a report on measures to reduce fatal youth assaults. The report highlighted the effect on young people of on-screen violence, and recommended the introduction of television V-chips, which block the reception of violent scenes. Television stations were asked to rate the violence contained in programs, and convenience stores were asked to make violent or other harmful magazines less accessible to children. The report stated that children's behavior is often the reflection of problems in the adult world; it advised parents to observe their children more carefully and called on schools to cooperate with local communities and the police. The promotion of counseling in schools was also recommended.

Anti-Drug Measures

According to a National Police Agency survey, the number of people arrested in 1997 for using stimulant drugs, specifically methamphetamines, increased for the third consecutive year to 19,937 nationwide. This figure included a record high of 262 middle and high school students, up 40 from the previous year.

In order to crack down on drug abuse, in 1998 the Japanese government decided on a five-year plan. Among the measures included in the plan are: police advice targeting minors on the street, police patrols delivering anti-drug messages in schools, and annual drug-abuse seminars held by police officers in middle and high schools. To further discourage drug abuse among youngsters, the government would carry out drug education programs not only in middle and high schools but also in elementary schools. Measures to rehabilitate drug addicts would also be implemented.

Because most drugs consumed in Japan are brought in illegally from abroad, the five-year plan called for concrete measures to stamp out foreign drug trafficking rings through international cooperation. The government would set out its anti-drug measures at a special session of the U.N. General Assembly beginning on June 8, 1998, at which U.N member countries would hold talks on the trafficking and abuse of illegal drugs and related issues.

Counseling

Truants, victims of bullying, returning students or others experiencing problems need counseling at school. Although students who have serious emotional or psychological problems are referred to an educational psychologist, in most cases, teachers function as counselors. Many teachers have little knowledge of counseling, and no professional training, yet they assume full responsibility for the students, and act as advisors.

To improve teachers' guidance skills, the Education Ministry prepares and distributes reference materials, while prefectural and municipal boards of education provide in-service teacher training. Schools experiencing particular difficulty in student guidance receive increased staff allocations. In the case of student guidance that requires knowledge in medicine and psychology, education centers and similar facilities run by boards of education in prefectures and municipalities provide advice to schools. In fiscal 1992, educational advice agencies totaled 254, the number of educational counselors was 1,670 and there were 123,198 cases involved in the provision of counseling nationwide. The Education Ministry also implements model programs to enhance educational counseling at the regional level.

Despite measures to help schools improve student guidance, the number of students in need of help has been increasing. The Education Ministry realizes the necessity of sending counselors directly to schools. In 1995, 154 counselors visited elementary and middle schools nationwide, to deal for the most part with truancy; in 1997 the number of counselors had risen to one thousand, and would be increased to 1,500 for the academic year beginning in April 1998. Nevertheless, the sheer number of elementary and middle schools (34,772 in fiscal 1996) means that for any counseling plan to be effective, there would have to be as many counselors as schools. Indeed, limited access to counseling is leading more and more students to visit school health clinics during regular class sessions. A survey conducted by the Education Ministry in the 1996 academic year found that 12 % of elementary schools and 37 % of middle schools had one or more students spending entire school days at the clinics, unable to go to their assigned classrooms.

It is clear, therefore, that school counseling is not widely accepted in Japan. There are two major reasons for this. Outside counselors are disliked by teachers since as third parties they may influence school activities and bring openness to the school, a closed society. On the other hand, teachers are neither equipped to act as counselors, nor do they have the time. As such, Japanese schools might do well to learn from the system in the United States, where teachers concentrate on teaching while communities set up a counseling system that sends counselors to schools and even kindergartens. The openness of American schools welcomes outside counselors and makes the system functional. For this to work in Japan however, the whole school hierarchy, and the culture of secrecy, would have to change.

Strong Leadership from the School Principal

Amid the series of knife crimes committed by middle and high school students, the Tokyo Metropolitan Board of Education decided in late February 1998 to boost the power of school principals by reducing the authority of teachers' assemblies. The board would revise its rules by specifying that the function of the assemblies is merely to support the principal. The revision, which would be in force in the 1998 school year, would allow principals to inspect students' bags or set class schedules at their discretion. Teachers' assemblies would no longer be able to overturn principals' decisions, or to vote on school policy.

The Education Ministry acknowledges in its 1994 White Paper that strong leadership by the principal is required for efficient school management. The improvement of school management under the principal's authority enables "teachers to apply their ideas and ingenuity to instruction and to ensuring an appropriate response to student guidance issues such as the refusal to attend school, bullying and school violence." The establishment of a structure in which all teaching staff and other personnel cooperate under the principal's direction also promotes "the appropriate enhancement of the apparatus for assigning duties among coordinating and advising teachers, maintenance of staff discipline, appropriate management of staff meetings and proper monitoring of the wishes of parents and other community residents."

This top-down structure requires able principals and deputy principals. The Education Ministry stresses the appointment of good administrators to these posts and recommends the promotion of capable younger teachers to such positions. Principals are allowed to extend their term of office in one school so that they can continue to exercise effective leadership.

Nevertheless, some education analysts have voiced concerns about the secondary status of teaching personnel and the definition of teachers' assemblies as supplementary bodies. It is thought that such measures may strengthen principals' discretionary power to the point where there is a risk of dictatorship within schools. Perhaps such powers are, anyway, unnecessary. In the United States school principals must earn the respect of staff and pupils whilst remaining "first among equals," working in co-operation with teachers and subject to reviews like all other school personnel.

A "Bill of Rights" in Tokorozawa High School

School principals' excessive discretionary power in Japanese schools was manifest in disputes between the head of the school and students at Tokorozawa High School, Saitama Prefecture, over the style of entrance and graduation ceremonies held in the 1997 and 1998 school years. The school principal, Tatsuo Uchida, held official school ceremonial events which included hoisting the national flag (*Hinomaru*) and singing the national anthem (*Kimikayo*) in accordance with the Education Ministry's course of study, the guideline on school curricula and related matters. However students boycotted the ceremonies, claiming that they undermined the trust between the principal and the students.

The students justified their unprecedented boycotting under the provisions of a "bill of rights," which they had established at a meeting in November 1990 and which invests a student council with certain decision-making powers and prevents school officials from forcing students to show respect to the flag and anthem. School authorities had been accepting the "bill of rights" and had agreed to set up mediation meetings to settle disputes over school policy between the student council and teaching staff.

Uchida's predecessors had held talks with student representatives when faculty decisions infringed on the bill. But when Uchida was appointed principal in April 1997, he held an entrance ceremony featuring the flag and anthem without consulting students or teachers. This display of autocracy enraged students and parents, who called for his resignation. At a meeting in November 1997, the students passed a resolution saying that they would organize their own graduation and entrance ceremonies. On March 9, 1998, most of the 420 graduating students boycotted a graduation ceremony planned by the principal, and attended a student-organized ceremony instead. Uchida refused to hold talks with the students, saying, "I'm not interested in a confrontation." He made every decision on school matters on his own without consulting others.

The Saitama Prefectural Board of Education upheld Uchida's decisions. After the graduation ceremonies, the board sent letters to parents of new students, requesting them to support an official entrance ceremony on April 9, 1998, led by the principal. The board also warned Tokorozawa High teachers about their planned talks with freshmen concerning the student-organized gathering for which the principal had not given his permission. In response, the teachers demanded that Uchida step down and that the admonition be nullified.

The principal maintained his hard-line policies: he sent freshmen and their parents letters stating that he would not admit new students to his school if they did not attend the official entrance ceremony. According to the Education Ministry, school principals have broad discretion on whether or not they admit students to a school. Nevertheless, this move angered parents, because students who had passed the entrance examination had already qualified for admission to the school. In the meantime, Tokorozawa High second- and third-year students were preparing for their own entrance ceremony, which was supported by a majority of the teachers.

On April 7, 1998, Education Minister Nobutaka Machimura announced that Tokorozawa High School should hold its next entrance ceremony under the leadership of the principal. The minister had been critical of the separate graduation ceremony sponsored by the students in March 1998. On April 9, the school's official entrance ceremony began at 9:40 a.m.: 154 of 398 freshmen did not attend. Uchida, however, backed down from his hard line policies and said that he would admit all the students including the 154, because of "educational considerations." In his speech, he urged the new students to study long and hard for a well-rounded education. The ceremony ended at 10:10 a.m., then all the students and most of the teachers participated in a second, student-organized ceremony, at which a student representative expressed gratitude to the teachers and the PTA, without whose help the event would not have been possible. He added that the ceremony was a special gift to all the freshmen.

Uchida said that there was no problem in holding two different entrance ceremonies; he only wished to hold a solemn ceremony based on the Education Ministry's guideline, which stipulates that school authorities plan entrance and graduation ceremonies as part of school activities and implement these events by hoisting the national flag and singing the national anthem. The Education Ministry commented that it was hard to understand why so many new students boycotted the school's ceremony despite the principal's permission for students to hold their own event. Many education analysts agreed that the escalation of discord or bad feelings would not resolve the problem, and advised that Uchida and the students resume their talks and take time to clarify their differences to reach an agreement.

The Tokorozawa High students did their best to protect their freedom and autonomy from the despotism of the principal, but as long as Uchida stuck to his conservative notion that students are subject to authorities regardless of circumstances, a constructive dialogue between them would be impossible. The students in the school could either stage a confrontation or they could give in to the principal. There was no "third way." Their revolt was exceptional. Students in most middle and high schools do not question the authority of school officials, but faithfully obey orders from teachers. Barred from assuming any responsibilities in school administration, they do not develop any free spirit or self-assertion, and rely heavily on adults. This lack of independent spirit enables teachers to adopt strict discipline and school rules that make students concentrate on studies and prevent them from making trouble at school.

Management of Schools by "Outsiders"

To revitalize the rigid education system, a subcommittee of the Central Council for Education, an advisory panel to the Education Minister, proposed on March 5, 1998 that the posts of school principal and head teacher be opened to candidates without teaching licenses. Under the present law five years of school teaching experience is required for appointment as principal or head teacher. (A similar move in 1996 had allowed 36 "outsiders" to take up full- and part-time teaching jobs.) Currently the excessive discretionary power of the principal reinforces the conventional pecking order at school and maintains the regimented and closed education system. The appointment of "outsiders" with a wide range of experience and knowledge may enhance learning, contribute to efficient school management, reduce school violence and other serious problems, and promote cooperation between the school, local community and households.

However, appointing principals who have neither teaching experience nor teaching licenses could disrupt staff management and damage the pride of the teaching personnel. Teachers, who fear the new plan might destroy the seniority system in which promotion and salary hikes depend on length of service, doubt that "outsiders" can handle school administration and school violence appropriately. It is likely that they will only tolerate "outsiders" who take up supplementary or part-time teaching positions.

The Authority of Local Boards of Education

Local boards of education intervene considerably in school administration. Therefore, "outsiders" appointed to top posts at school may have little room for maneuver. In the rigid Japanese education system, just as school principals control ordinary teachers, so local boards of education wield power over control principals. Local boards in Hiroshima Prefecture, for instance, demand that principals in public schools submit a list of teaching materials (supplementary readers, manuals, reference books, workbooks, etc) for approval. While the boards claim that this ensures that only good teaching materials are used, some analysts argue that such restrictions curtail the freedom of teachers and the principals' authority over school management.

Field trip destinations are also examined by local boards of education. In May 1998, the board of education of Matsubara, Osaka, ordered Matsubara Sixth Junior High School to change its planned trip to Okinawa. Most students and teachers believed that it would be educationally valuable to visit this island, the scene of intense battles in the spring of 1945, which took the lives of more than 200,000 soldiers and civilians and where large U.S. military bases are now sited. The board claimed that it was not politically neutral to take students to sites such as the Kadena U.S. Air Base while there were controversies over the existence of U.S military bases in Japan. Perhaps the board was afraid that students might develop anti-base sentiments. The school had no choice but to change the excursion's Itinerary. Some prefectures even restrict the means of transportation for school trips. For example, the Tochigi Municipal Board of Education, Tochigi Prefecture, although providing no satisfactory explanations, bans school excursions by air, so all students in that prefecture have to go on long trips by bus or train.

The Authority of the Education Ministry

Politics and education are firmly linked in Japan, with the local boards of education subject to the Education Ministry. In the case of Matsubara Sixth Junior High School's planned trip to Okinawa, the board of education had to make a decision in line with the government policy supporting the Japan-U.S. security treaty. The ruling Liberal Democratic Party wants to keep students ignorant of U.S military bases in Japan to minimize anti-base sentiment.

Any local boards that do not conform to the government's education policies are reprimanded. On May 21, 1998, the Education Ministry admonished the Hiroshima Board of Education following a survey it had conducted in April. The survey had found that only 36.3 % of elementary schools, 35.8 % of middle schools and 22.0 % of high schools sang the national anthem in the 1998 entrance ceremony. When the city of Hiroshima was totally destroyed, with the death of tens of thousands, by the atomic bomb dropped by a U.S airplane on August 9, 1945, the national flag, *Hinomaru,* and anthem, *Kimigayo,* were symbols of Japanese militarism. Some members of the LDP, however, still glorify the war and try to instill nationalism and patriotism in school children. Thus the Ministry insists that boards ensure compliance with its Course of Study, requiring public schools to sing the anthem and hoist the flag in a prominent position. The public schools in Hiroshima Prefecture, with the connivance of the local board, probably disobeyed out of respect for the dead and distrust of nationalism. In some schools, students were even taught that *Kimigayo* was not the national anthem and that *Hinomaru* was not the national flag.

The superintendent of the board of education said, "I am sorry for not recognizing the situation. The board will devote time to the issue and sincerely persuade schools to follow the Course of Study... But I cannot guarantee to rectify all of the problems." The Ministry also reprimanded the board for allowing middle schools to conduct 45-minute lessons, rather than the stipulated 50 minutes, and complained that in 43 schools "moral education" was called "human rights education."

Moral Education and Home Training

The Japanese education authorities believe that moral education is imperative to reduce school problems, especially delinquency. In 1998, "Moral Education from Childhood," an interim report by the Central Council for Education (an advisory panel to the Education Minister), claimed that declining moral standards in adults - self-centeredness, dissipation, money worship and irresponsibility - were partly responsible for the alarming number of crimes committed by youths. The report recommends that teachers stand firm against disruptive students at school, and that they cooperate with the police if necessary. School principals are responsible for requesting police patrols in schools and reporting school violence to juvenile crime officials. The report suggests that educators and parents protect children from violent television programs and videos. Indeed, the report made unprecedented recommendations for the discipline of children in the home for the sake of their sound emotional and moral development.

The Chairman of the Central Council for Education explained that although it was the parents who were responsible for raising their children, many parents thought that all they needed to do was feed, clothe and send children off to school where they expected teachers to guide their moral development. Therefore,

162

while the government should not intervene in the home, it must advise parents that strict discipline should be adopted from a very young age. Parents should distinguish right from wrong, scold their children for bad behavior and set up rules on family matters, for example that children must help with household chores. Children would then realize that there are rules in the world that must be obeyed. The report especially calls for fathers' active involvement in home discipline, suggesting that working hours should be cut to allow workers time to educate their children. Mothers can become female role models for their daughters, but only fathers can teach sons about social responsibilities. In a recent survey only 7.8% of fathers said that they conducted home training, compared with 81.5 % of mothers.

The report, however, suggests that parents should not over-protect their children, otherwise the children will stop thinking independently and will not work out problems on their own. It warns parents against letting their children attend private cram schools or hiring private tutors, stressing that hours of intensive study every day could lead to unbalanced development, depriving children of playtime and opportunities for socializing and community activities.

In April 1998, the Education Ministry decided to compile a "Handbook on Home Discipline," based on the interim report, to be delivered to about 4.8 million households nationwide in the fall of 1998. It is unlikely, however, that the interim report or the "Handbook on Home Discipline" will be effective. Unfortunately, education does not begin at home in Japan, unlike in western countries. In a survey of 2,047 parents and teachers in public elementary and middle schools in Tochigi Prefecture conducted by the Tochigi Economic Association from January to April 1997, about 80 % of parents said that teachers should shoulder responsibility for moral education. Of the parents polled, 56.3 % wanted schools to teach children politeness and consideration for others, and 23.8 % compliance with the law and participation in volunteer work. On the other hand 78 % of teachers said that parents were responsible for moral education, and 85.5 % stated that they did not teach morality in class, contrary to the class schedule and teaching guidelines. Fifty-eight percent of teachers said that children lacked a moral sense appropriate to their age. While 31.8 % attributed this to "a number of children who have no understanding of human relationships," 41.8 % blamed "the increasing number of parents who lack a sense of morality."

Based on the results of the survey, the association recommended that the prefectural governor set up "Seminars on Moral Education" for young parents and "Counseling on Child Care" in local governments. It also urged kindergartens and nursery schools to reserve a room for the counseling of mothers, and to suggest that more parental involvement in school would enhance the healthy progress of children.

Confucianism

In order to understand why Japanese parents renounce their responsibilities as moral educators and instead turn to the authorities, it is necessary to understand the impact of Confucianism on Japanese society, and in particular, how it has helped to mold the Japanese education system.

Confucianism is represented by the *Analects of Confucius* (551-478 B.C), a set of lessons featuring a harmonious world in which children are devoted to their parents and respectful of their elders. In this world children can gain good will by being dutiful to their families and by respecting their responsibilities and promises; they must study hard, absorb all they are taught, and not tire of learning. Teachers also have a responsibility never to get tired of teaching.

On a larger scale, the state ruler gains respect by showing devotion to his parents and by treating his subjects solemnly. The people will obey him as long as he selects virtuous men to control the dishonest, but not if he chooses corrupt men to oversee the honest. People lay down their lives by serving virtuous rulers, resulting in the creation of the world of harmony.

Confucius' emphasis on good will, virtue and responsibility is highly relevant to the Education Ministry's emphasis on moral education. In Confucianism, people are subject to virtuous rulers who take care of them in every respect. Similarly, parents submit themselves to the ministry on behalf of their children. Taking the place of parents, the ministry teaches children morals in a systematic education system in order to deter school violence and other youth crimes. The ministry controls education both at school and in the home, because in the Confucian world view, public and private matters are the same.

Thus the school and home assume the world of harmony. Children obey their (virtuous) teachers and parents; they have a responsibility to work hard, and as long as they fulfil their duties, they are called good children. In this world, students are not allowed to have individual freedom, which may motivate them to disobey teachers or break school rules. To deny individualism and contain various school problems, school officials adopt severe school rules and other similar measures. School ceremonies meanwhile, are a reflection of the Confucian emphasis on rituals as vital for driving away enemies and dispelling sickness. The solemn ceremonies at school may be means of keeping children away from temptation, and inclining them toward studies and learning.

Education of Japanese Children Living Abroad and Returnees

As Japan's role on the international scene increases, the number of Japanese children in the compulsory education age group who are living abroad on a long-term basis is on the rise: in fiscal 1994 the number stood at approximately 50,000. To meet the needs of these children, by fiscal 1994 local Japanese residents' associations and other groups had established 90 full-time schools and 167 supplementary education schools worldwide, and school corporations in Japan had founded 16 private overseas educational facilities. The Education Ministry sends both full and part-time teachers to these schools, provides teaching equipment, distributes free textbooks and designates a number of schools in Japan as pilot schools to conduct studies on Japanese education overseas. Through the Japan Overseas Educational Services, the ministry also offers counseling services to children going abroad with their parents, as well as correspondence education programs for Japanese children overseas.

Every year about 10,000 children return to Japanese elementary, middle, and high schools from abroad. The ministry takes measures to ensure the returning students' successful re-entry into Japanese schools: it sets up special classes in schools affiliated with national universities for those whose Japanese proficiency is insufficient to attend normal classes, and it designates pilot schools to cooperate in research on education for these children. The ministry also promotes the education of returning students by encouraging high schools and universities to reserve a specific number of places for them.

Japanese children living in other countries know that high school and university entrance exams in Japan are highly competitive. Thus, they turn to private cram schools in the countries where they are temporarily resident, in order to pass the exams when they return to Japan. When these children reenter a school in Japan, however, practices in class may seem strange to them, and they are perplexed by the way they are treated. In particular, returnees wonder why there are few discussions and why they are rarely called on to answer questions. They may also be uncomfortable with the requirement to eat lunch quickly, and the stipulation that no one is allowed to leave the classroom until everybody in the group finishes eating.

Most schools do not offer returning children a warm reception, nor do they regard them as promoters of international understanding. There is no celebration of difference in Japanese schools. If the children do not speak fluent Japanese, they are treated like outsiders or aliens, just as physically or mentally disabled children are. They face a lot of pressure to conform to the established school order, for doing the same thing at the same time as everyone else is one of the characteristics of Japanese schools. If returnees do not want to be ostracized, they need to assimilate quickly. This process may be difficult, and children may need counseling to help them adjust; in most cases however, this is not available.

An Academic Survey on the State of International Exchange in High Schools

Since the 1986 school year, the Education Ministry has conducted biennial surveys on the state of international exchange in high schools. The 1994 survey, released on February 7, 1995, found an increase in the number of students going overseas and of foreign students coming to Japan.

In the 1994 school year, 374 schools (113 public, 261 private) conducted school excursions to foreign countries, with the participation of 95,010 students, up 31.7 % from the last survey. Popular destinations were Korea, China and the USA. Students who studied abroad for more than three months totaled 3,998

(1,880 public and 2,118 private school students), an 11 % rise. The USA was the most popular destination, followed by Australia, Canada and New Zealand, among over 49 countries. The number of students who participated in a short-term study program abroad stood at 32,465, a 0.5 % rise. The most popular destination was the USA, followed by Australia, New Zealand and Canada.

Foreign students who came to Japan totaled 1,143 (491 public and 652 private school students), a 5 % increase. They were accepted by 818 schools. Students came most often from Australia, followed by the USA, Canada and New Zealand, among 43 participating countries. The types of students were: 640 auditors, 391 regular students and 112 others.

Chapter 5: High Schools

The percentage of students continuing to study beyond the compulsory level has risen steadily, from about 40 % soon after World War II to 50 % in the mid-1950s, 70 % in the mid-1960s and over 90 % in the mid-1970s. In fiscal 1994 the percentage stood at 96.5 %, and had risen to 96.7 % in fiscal 1995. Once enrolled, students rarely drop out: in 1991 the percentage of students quitting high school before graduation was only about 2 %. High schools are now all but part of the compulsory education system.

Middle school students who choose not to go on to high school can enter the job market. However parents are generally opposed to this option, on the grounds that people who do not have a high school degree are at a disadvantage in society. Companies look for workers with good academic backgrounds, and consequently, middle school graduates are unable to get good jobs, regardless of their abilities. The same goes for marriage: well-educated women are reluctant to marry men with lesser school degrees, and the balance of academic degrees between bride and groom is very important.

School Rules

High schools maintain the same rigid discipline found in middle schools. Students wear uniforms and are subject to strict school rules. Disruptive students are reprimanded or may even be subject to corporal punishment. In high schools, however, discipline and pressure to study are not offset with entertainment. There are few school excursions or athletic meetings, and classes do not feature the colorful aids to learning found in elementary and middle schools. The high school is totally focused on studies.

To maintain an optimal atmosphere for study, high schools even prescribe what students are and are not allowed to do out of school. For example, a number of high schools prohibit students from gaining a motorcycle license or driving motorcycles, on the grounds that time spent driving motorcycles is time wasted, when students should be studying. Similarly, many high schools forbid students to work, thus depriving students of valuable social experience and a first step toward independence. This prohibition directly contradicts Article 22 of the Constitution of Japan, ensuring freedom of occupation.

Students do not defy oppressive school policies. They neither file suit against the school for damages caused by strict school rules, nor do they call for the abolition of such rules. There would be little chance of winning a suit since judges usually side with the schools. Moreover, in Japan, trials take years to come to judgement, by which time plaintiffs (students) would have become adults and the merit of the litigation would have disappeared. Severe school rules therefore remain steadfast, supported by judges and by the majority of people.

Allowances

Whilst students are subject to strict discipline at school, outside school hours generous allowances allow young people a large amount of freedom. According to a survey conducted by the Japan Youth Research Institute, in 1997 68 % of teenagers received a regular allowance, about ¥20,000 ($165) a month on average. Students spend this money on leisure activities, to find an outlet for the stress caused by severe discipline at school.

However the freedom allowed by large allowances is largely illusory. Although students can live well without going out to work, they come to rely too much on their parents, and do not develop their independence. In some cases children are given an allowance in return for studying, which again inhibits the development of mental autonomy.

Single-Gender Education

Single-gender high schools are thought to provide students with a good atmosphere for study. Despite moves in Japan towards enhanced equal rights for men and women, conservative school officials have argued for the maintenance of traditional single-gender schools, claiming that students in co-ed schools may be distracted by the presence of the opposite sex, and fail to concentrate on their studies. In single-gender schools, students can achieve their maximum potential and produce good academic results. Girls especially have more confidence, feel freer to express themselves, develop a potential for leadership and improve their test scores, specifically in math and science. Single-gender schools also make it less likely that teenagers will start dating, a pursuit frowned upon by school officials, teachers and parents, many of whom favor strict separation of the sexes, disapproving even of male and female students walking to school together. Consequently, a majority of students rarely date in couples, and are not sexually experienced.

Nevertheless, the argument for single-gender schools may already have been lost. In fiscal 1949, 42.2 % of all public high schools in Japan were single-gender schools, but by May 1997 the figure had fallen to 4.2 %.

Female Students and Science

Japanese high school students have a limited number of elective courses. There is a marked difference in the choice of elective subjects between male and female students. Girls select humanities: English, Japanese, social studies, etc., rather than sciences: physics, chemistry, biology. It is noticeable that this preference is not present in the early school years, when girls show as much interest in science as boys, and indeed, some education analysts attribute girls' disinclination towards science to gender stereotypes, which are reinforced as children get older. To break down these stereotypes, parents and teachers need to persuade girls to study science in order to pursue careers as scientists or engineers, instead of blocking them from seeking nontraditional careers.

Yet, lest we make too hasty a conclusion, it is necessary to take into consideration the "story-telling" nature of women. While men prefer performance or competition-oriented jobs, women favor "story-telling" jobs, or careers involved in human relationships. Women want to be doctors or teachers rather than engineers or computer scientists, social workers or secretaries rather than technicians or repairpersons, and salespersons or hairdressers rather than builders or truck drivers. In short, they like to work in a human-oriented rather than a machine- or result-oriented environment. Therefore, it would be difficult to encourage many schoolgirls to study science for careers in technology, even if a world of equal opportunity could be guaranteed.

Types of High Schools and Study Programs

High schools are of two types: general and vocational. General high schools offer general study programs, specialized study programs (math, science, English, etc) and vocational study programs (agricultural, industrial, commercial, fishery, home economics, nursing, etc). Students majoring in general programs typically take Japanese, mathematics, social studies, science, English, home economics, physical education, health, and music or art. Students majoring in science take more science subjects (integral and differential calculus, statistics, probability, physics, chemistry, etc) than subjects in the humanities. Students who are English majors take more subjects in English. Those enrolled in vocational programs take subjects related to their majors. Vocational high schools offer vocational programs, and a typical vocational high school is either a commercial, technical or agricultural high school. Some schools offer part-time and correspondence programs to employees who want to receive a high school education while working.

The timetable in full-time high schools is tight. There are four 50-minutes lessons in the morning and two in the afternoon from Monday through Friday; and four lessons in the morning on Saturday. Japanese students do not enjoy the flexibility afforded in American schools. There are no self-study periods in which to prepare for the next class or try to finish their homework, and while students in American high schools have individual schedules, Japanese students all take the same subjects at the same times, and have lunch at their own desks in the homeroom classroom at 12:30 p.m.

Like middle school students, full-time Japanese high school students take two mid-term and three end-of-term exams in a school year. There are also a number of other tests and trial exams. Teachers believe that the more they give tests, the more students will study.

Students study many different subjects, some of which are unrelated to daily lives or chosen careers. Whilst they understand the importance of Japanese and foreign languages, many students wonder why they must study advanced math, chemistry or ancient history, for example: knowledge of these subjects is hardly a prerequisite for success in the business world. In order to tackle this problem, Japanese schools might need to provide students with more elective courses so that they can choose subjects according to their interests and needs. However, they must keep in mind the aim of general education, lest high schools become vocational training centers. Students acquire a wide range of knowledge by taking many subjects in both science and the humanities. By doing so, they become cultured, one of the main goals of general education.

General Study Programs

General study programs have been gaining in popularity over the other programs, because they provide an advantage when it comes to preparation for university entrance exams. In the 1960s, about 60 % of students enrolled in general programs, but by 1996 that percentage had risen to approximately 74 %. For a student enrolled on a general program, a typical week's schedule consists of four hours each of English, Japanese and math, three hours each of world history, geography, chemistry, biology and physical education, two hours each of music, art and home economics, an hour of homeroom and other subjects.

In their second year at high school students are required to choose either science-mathematics or literature as the field of concentration for the final year. This allows them to focus on university entrance exams, the subjects for which differ from department to department. Students applying for science and engineering courses specialize in science-mathematics, while students intending to apply to humanities departments specialize in literature and take more English, Japanese and social science classes.

Most high-performing students go on to competitive universities, and average or below-average students often apply to non-competitive universities, vocational colleges or junior colleges. Recently, the college entrance ratio has been rising: in fiscal 1997, 47.3 % of high school students went on to a higher education.

Students who want to work upon graduation use employment placement services at school, whereby the homeroom teacher advises them on how to take an employment test and interview. Approximately 19 % of graduates of general study programs enter the work force upon graduation each year.

Vocational Study Programs

Vocational high schools and a majority of general high schools offer vocational study programs designed for those who wish to obtain practical jobs upon graduation. For example, students majoring in commercial studies take bookkeeping, typing, accounting and computer science, besides general subjects; students majoring in technical, agricultural or other programs take subjects in related fields. These programs tend to attract the least academic students, since the entrance examinations are less competitive than those for general study programs. It is not surprising then, given the hierarchical nature of Japanese education, that students enrolled in vocational programs are regarded as inferior to those majoring in general programs.

Although graduates of vocational programs are more or less guaranteed a job, recently more and more of them have gone on to vocational college, junior college or university. Most vocational colleges and junior colleges are non-competitive, but those who want to enter a competitive university have to study long and hard.

Part-time Study Programs

Part-time study programs offer general education courses in the evenings. The programs last four years, and students must attend regularly in order to graduate. The part-time high schools are non-competitive, their only entrance requirement being a middle-school degree, and therefore attract students who have failed in their high school entrance exams, as well as those independent-minded students who wish to complete their high school education without being financially dependent on their parents.

Whilst vocational courses are considered inferior to general courses, evening high schools are even lower down the hierarchy, regarded as third-rate schools attended only by slow learners, repeaters or dropouts. Not surprisingly therefore, students with average scholastic abilities are unwilling to go to this type of school.

Reforms on Flexibility in High School Education

The Education Ministry has recognized that the inflexibility of the high school education system stymies schools' freedom of education and development of students' autonomy. Therefore, in March 1989, the ministry's Course of Study for high schools was amended, with amendments coming into force in April 1994. The ministry's 1994 White Paper explains the aims of the reform.

> The new Course of Study is designed to provide solutions to a variety of issues facing high school education; to anticipate social change, including the advent of an era of lifelong learning; and to improve high school education. The main goals of the Course of Study are to foster the willingness to learn independently and the ability to cope positively with social change, to enhance the ability of

181

education to develop individuality, and to enhance education regarding the requirements of a fully human life and approaches to life. In addition to the improvement of educational content in order to respond appropriately to students' diverse needs and to social change, the Course of Study calls for the encouragement of educational activities that utilize the ideas, ingenuity, and distinctive characteristics of individual schools....

The new Course of Study gives priority to the basic aspects of education essential for life as a citizen of Japan. This emphasis is reflected in the increased care with which the content of subject areas and subjects is selected, while efforts are being made to maintain consistency with middle school education. Priority is also given to the development of various abilities, including thought, judgment, and self-expression, through various subject areas and subjects, and to the encouragement of scholastic activities that foster students' creativity and imagination, such as exploratory activities, project studies, and theme-oriented learning.

The revised Course of Study stipulates the following measures: establishment of comprehensive general courses; restructuring of subject areas and subjects; introduction of inter-school cooperation including permission for cross-studying between general and vocational high schools; and facilitation of transfers between schools and courses.

In the past, students had been unable to change their majors once they entered a high school, because the selection of applicants is done on a departmental basis. To rectify this, a comprehensive course program was established to allow students to declare a major *after* being admitted to school, and to enable them to complete either a general, specialized or vocational course of study. Forty-five schools nationwide have adopted this program. The Education Ministry also recommended that schools increase the number of options available to students.

The Course of Study improved educational content by restructuring subject areas and subjects to meet the needs of a changing society and environments. It expanded 45 subjects in eight subject areas to 62 subjects in nine subject areas in general programs; and 157 subjects in six subject areas to 184 subjects in six subject areas in vocational (specialized) programs. Schools were also permitted to establish subject areas and subjects other than those specified in the Course of Study, and to vary the length of class sessions to meet the specific needs of learning each subject. To ease students' workloads, the standard curriculum for subject areas and subjects in full-day programs called for 35 weeks of instruction per year.

Under the new provisions, "social studies" was reorganized into two subjects: "geography and history" and "civics." World history became a compulsory subject. In the subject area of foreign language (English), "oral/aural communication A, B and C" were established to develop communication skills through speech and conversation in everyday situations. A new science subject was introduced: "integrated science," which covers a basic knowledge of physics, chemistry, biology and geology, and is intended to "[foster] a scientific way of perceiving and thinking through research and project studies on the natural environment" (1994 White Paper). The emphasis was "on exploratory approaches to topics that are relevant to everyday life such as resources and energy, environmental protection and biotechnology."

In general programs, new subjects such as information, welfare and the tourist industry were recommended in view of the network society, aging society, and the prospect of tourism in the 21st century. In vocational programs, information-related subjects were expanded to deal with changing industrial environments. Composite courses such as agricultural economics and electronic engineering were offered as standard courses, and project studies were introduced to develop problem-solving skills and creativity.

High schools have also undergone reforms designed to reflect the changing roles of the sexes within society. Whereas previously, only girls took courses on home economics, these courses are now compulsory for both male and female students. According to the 1994 White Paper, this is to ensure that they "are equipped with the skills that they will need to survive in an era of an 80-year life expectancy, and to enable them to acquire the knowledge and techniques needed to create a fulfilling family lifestyle."

Where rules are implemented strictly and rigidly, students who fail in a subject are not allowed to advance to the next grade. However the Education Ministry intends to prevent students from dropping out because they have failed a grade. The Course of Study stipulates, "Students should be treated as flexibly as possible. Instead of requiring students to repeat grades under a uniform system, provision should be made for them to graduate provided that they can accumulate the required number of credits by the time of graduation." Indeed, the credit-based system is promoted by the ministry, and in April 1994 there were 55 credit-based high schools.

Iwayado High School

Among the various education reforms proposed by the government, it is the choice-centered curriculum that most enhances schools' freedom of education and students' autonomy. Let us take as an example Iwayado High School, Iwate Prefecture, which in 1994 adopted a five-class integrated-program based on the choice-centered curriculum.

First-year students in Iwayado High School take "Japanese language I," "mathematics I," "world history A," "physical education," "health," "general home economics," and "industrial society and human beings" as compulsory subjects. They also choose subjects from "civics," "science" and "art" as compulsory electives; that is, students must select subjects from each of these subject areas. In this first year curriculum, the number of free elective subjects is limited.

In the second year, the number of compulsory subjects is reduced to four: "physical education," "health," "general home economics" and "basic information." Compulsory electives are chosen from among the subject areas of "history," "geography" and "science." Students can select other elective subjects according to their own interests and concerns. In the third year, the only compulsory subjects are "physical education" and "project study." There are no compulsory electives.

Student Transfers

In the past, it was difficult for students to transfer between high schools. Little information was available on opportunities and procedures for transfers, and transfer students had to pass entrance exams in five subjects: Japanese language, foreign languages (English), math, social sciences and science. The Education Ministry has tried to address these problems, in order to make the education system more flexible.

Since 1984, the Education Ministry has repeatedly urged prefectural governments to expand school entrance opportunities, administer simple and flexible entrance exams and establish special entrant quotas. In response to these recommendations, most schools have started to admit transfer students based on scholastic test scores in three subjects (the Japanese language, foreign languages and math) instead of five, and on interviews.

The ministry has also developed the "School Transfer Information System," which enables students to obtain latest information on transfer admission from prefectural boards of education, prefectural government departments that supervise private schools, the National Education Center, or other relevant organizations. Since February 1992, information on transfer admission has been distributed to schools through the "Admission Information System of the High School Transfer Student," which connects the National Education Center with prefectural boards of education and other organizations across the country via a computer network.

Despite efforts simplifying transfer admission processes, however, the number of transfer students is still relatively low - about 8,600 in fiscal 1989 and around 11,800 in fiscal 1991.

College-Bound Students in Competitive High Schools

Competitive high schools are at the zenith of the "rank order" of high schools. They accept only the brightest middle school students and train them to be admitted to prestigious universities. High-performing students can gain almost perfect scores in the standard entrance exam held by average universities, but top universities give more complex exams in order to select only the best applicants. Therefore, the competitive schools use higher quality textbooks than do average schools, with more difficult and complex questions. Teachers teach only materials relevant to exam questions, and coach students in problem-solving techniques. In math classes for example, students practice solving difficult questions on progression, matrixes, vector functions, trigonometric functions, differential calculus and integral calculus, so that they can handle actual exam questions with ease. Humanities students on the other hand are not required to develop analytical abilities, since memorization of factual knowledge is the key to high exam scores.

Students who do well in class achievement tests are praised, and their names and scores are put on a list on the bulletin board in the classroom: these are the students expected to go on to the most famous universities. This ranking system inevitably stimulates competition among students, and urges them to work harder to surpass their peers. Many college-bound students study many hours a day, holding to the motto "pass with four, fail with five," meaning that if students sleep as much as five hours a day, they will flunk their entrance exams.

Reasons for Self-sacrifice

College-bound students make many sacrifices, studying long and hard to pass the entrance exam of a famous university. There are three reasons for this self-denial: diplomaism, Confucianism and conservatism.

Deplomaism means that higher academic backgrounds are important to securing a profession and building up a career. In Japan, many companies judge and hire newcomers according to the university from which they graduate: leading corporations look for graduates from top universities, while non-competitive university students are usually hired by mid-sized or small companies, and are thus unable to join the elite.

The influence of Confucianism in Japanese society means that admission to a competitive university implies "honor," while failure in an exam indicates "disgrace." Unlike the United States, where failure is temporary and you can try again, in Japan students

189

have much more at stake: they are trying to gain fame and avoid humiliation. Furthermore, because group interests are placed above individual endeavors, children are urged to concentrate on their studies for the fame of the family and school. Personal goals are assimilated with filial duty - children's success is identical to the family's accomplishment. Hence, the concepts of responsibility and personal goals remain foreign to Japanese children, who belong to their parents rather than to themselves. Children's individual freedom is maintained under the protection of parents, whose ideas and decisions are supposed to be excellent and beneficial. At school, children have obligations to their school and teachers, whose instruction and judgement are supposed to be the best. Students who pass the entrance exam of a famous university are celebrated as contributors to the enhancement of the school's reputation. This philosophy assumes that all individuals can be successful if they try hard; no allowance is made for innate ability, and students' failure in exams is attributed to a lack of effort. The idea that "you can do it if you try" results in *Jukensenso* (examination preparation war) and in *Jukenjigoku* (examination hell), which many people take as a matter of course.

Another reason for the Japanese people's adherence to their rigid education system may be their conservatism and ignorance of education systems in other countries. Most Japanese teachers do not know much about different education values and systems, so they believe that the Japanese way is the only legitimate method of education. Traditional education values are so deeply rooted in society that educators have little incentive to go abroad to observe different systems, or to read literature on educational reform. Moreover, Japanese schools, teachers and parents always look to the government for leadership in educational reform - there is no grass-roots movement. Under these circumstances, it is impossible either to clarify or to rectify the problems inherent in Japanese education.

Selection of the University

University applicants and their families select potential universities in consultation with their homeroom teachers or other specialists, who counsel them on their chances of entering colleges based on their achievement or other standard test scores. Teachers also use these test scores as a guideline in career guidance; for example, those who do well on math and science tests are advised to take entrance exams to engineering departments, and those who perform well on English and Japanese tests are recommended to major in humanities.

Many students take the entrance exams of several competitive and non-competitive universities, as an insurance policy in case they fail to enter the university of their first choice. Applicants who fail to pass any of the entrance exams they take usually apply again the following year.

University Entrance Exams

Admission to public, and a few private, universities requires applicants to sit a two-tiered entrance exam. Preliminary exams, a sort of uniform national college admission test, are held in mid-January by the participating universities, in cooperation with the National Center for University Entrance Examinations (NCUEE). The second-stage exams are held by the individual universities in early March. Entrance exams for most private universities are administered in February. Opportunities to apply to national universities are limited, since all schedule their exams on the same dates. Local public universities and private universities set their exams on different dates, so students can take dozens of such entrance exams.

Preliminary exams are intended to evaluate applicants' basic academic achievement, and are prepared and marked exclusively by the NCUEE. Questions are all multiple-choice, developed in conformity with the national curriculum by dozens of different subject area committees, which ensure that questions are consistent and uniform in style and difficulty. The exams are constantly reviewed and revised. The NCUEE claims that students who study authorized textbooks on a regular basis can answer at least 70 % of the questions correctly.

In the 1997 school year, first-stage entrance exams were held on January 17 and 18, 1998, simultaneously at 562 locations throughout the country. A total of 597,271 people took the two-day test, and were able to choose subjects in six subject-areas, with 34 subcategories, depending on the requirements of the university to which they were applying. Students applying to famous universities such as Tokyo University are usually required to take four to seven subjects from the subject areas of English, Japanese, math and social studies and science, while applicants to other universities typically take fewer subjects.

The number of applicants is approximately three times higher than the number of students the universities can accept. Therefore, applicants with low scores in the first-stage exam are not allowed to take the second round. To reduce the workload involved in handling a large body of applicants some universities establish a cutoff point and fail candidates who fall below that point. Tokyo

University turns down about 3,000 applicants, or about 25 % of the total in this screening each year.

The second-stage exams are conducted by individual universities. Test subjects are determined at the discretion of each institution, and they differ from school to school and from department to department within the same university. For the prestigious universities in particular, exam questions are complex and challenging. The top-ranking Tokyo University sets the most difficult exams, in order to select only the highest achieving students from among straight A applicants.

The results of first and second-stage exams are used in appropriate combination in order to select students suitable for the education each university provides. In most cases second-stage exam scores are counted equal to preliminary exam scores, but in competitive universities the emphasis is on the second stage exams, since high performing applicants can be expected to achieve almost perfect scores on first-stage exams.

The outcome of entrance exams is mailed to examinees or put on the bulletin boards in the universities. On the day when results are announced, most examinees go to the university and gather in front of large bulletin boards on which the seat numbers of successful candidates are written. Those who find their number on the list rush to share the news and to celebrate, while unsuccessful applicants are devastated. The results of university entrance exams are considered as a sort of climax in one's life.

The University Entrance Qualification Exam

Students who have completed or expect to complete a high school program are entitled to apply to a university. Recently, as part of its educational reforms, the Education Ministry has extended this entitlement to those who do not have a high school graduation certificate, provided that they are at least 18 years old and pass a university entrance qualification exam that tests their basic level of academic achievement in English, Japanese, math, science, social studies and other high school subjects.

It is not easy for students to prepare for university entrance qualification exams by themselves. Most go to a private preparatory school, a sort of *juku*, to improve their scholastic abilities. After passing the exams, and thus meeting university entrance qualifications, students apply to a university and take university entrance exams.

Reform of University Entrance Exams

In 1990 the Joint First-Stage Achievement Test (JFSAT) for university entrance was replaced by a more flexible and diversified system, the NCUEE exams. The new program allows each university to choose its exam format and requirements, for example entrance exams without math or English tests or including only one or two subjects are permitted. Under the old JFSAT system, all applicants to all universities had to take seven subjects, three from the areas of foreign languages, Japanese and math (200 points per subject) and four from the sciences and social studies (100 points per subject), giving a total score out of 1,000. Each applicant could only apply to one university, to which the test results were sent. The new system permits multiple applications to a wider range of universities - the old system had excluded most private universities.

The NCUEE exams also aim to counter the JFSAT's excessive emphasis on academic abilities by promoting criteria that meet the objectives and characteristics of each university and department, and allow for a multifold evaluation of each applicant's abilities and aptitudes. The Education Ministry recommends that universities utilize a variety of selection methods: school reports on a student's grades and conduct, interviews, essay tests, proficiency tests, practical skills tests, extracurricular (volunteer) activities, and personal recommendations. Universities are also advised to establish special selection quotas for returning and mature students.

A further problem with the JFSAT exams was their effect on university ranking. Universities were judged according to the average exam score of its successful applicants. For example, students at a prestigious top university might average 900 points out of 1,000, while a less fashionable university's candidates might average 600. As the most academically gifted opted for the top universities the differential continuously increased. However, while an increasing number of universities have adopted different entrant selection methods in accordance with the Education Ministry's suggestions, the top-ranked universities still rely almost exclusively on entrance exam scores and continue to demand excessively high academic standards from their applicants.

Perhaps the Education Ministry believed that incorporating elements from the American admission system, in which a student's attendance, grades, personal recommendations and volunteer activities are all counted more or less equally with exam scores, might reduce the academic burden and pressure on Japanese students. However, a foreign education system cannot easily be imposed on a country with a different culture, social structure, religion and history. In Japan, Confucianism, which obliges children to study hard, disinclines universities to introduce an Anglo-Saxon-style university admission system. A number of education reform panels of the Education Ministry are currently holding intensive discussions on educational reforms modeled on the American education system, but the proposals are meeting with strong opposition from those who fear they threaten the traditional Japanese virtue of hard and long study.

Ronin and *Yobiko*

Many university applicants take the entrance exams of several universities. If they fail all the exams, they either try again the following year, go on to a non-competitive (vocational) college, or look for a job. Those who choose to retake the exams are called *ronin*, literally "masterless" wandering *samurai* (warriors), a warlike term that reflects the intensity of *Jukensenso* (examination preparation war). Students who are not accepted by the university of their first choice often decide to become *ronin*, even if they pass the exams of the other universities to which they have applied, because a diploma from a famous university is more attractive. In all, *ronin* account for about 15% of this age group.

The *romin* has to wait a year for another chance, since university entrance exams are held only once a year in winter for the academic year starting in April. While many male students do not mind becoming *ronin*, a number of female students are reluctant to wait another year, and enter non-competitive universities or junior colleges instead.

In March and April, hundreds of thousands of unsuccessful university applicants apply to *yobiko*, private schools for the preparation of university entrance exams. Most are accepted, although famous prep schools screen out applicants by setting entrance exams that are often as difficult as those of prestigious universities. The best *yobiko* teach good test-taking strategies, more or less guaranteeing their students' success in the most competitive university entrance exams. Teaching methods are similar to those used in top high schools: rote learning, training in test-taking skills, etc. Because university entrance exams are similar in format and content each year, *yobiko* instructors develop an anticipated exam for each university by analyzing its exams from several previous years, and students practice on the expected exam questions of the universities of their choice. Students also learn how to memorize factual knowledge effectively in order to answer exam questions. If there is an essay question on an exam, prep schools provide attendees with a writing course. It is not surprising therefore that *Yobiko* attendees are at an advantage in passing university entrance exams. Every year, approximately 50

% of applicants accepted by Tokyo University, the most prestigious Japanese public university, and by Keio University and Waseda University, the most sought after private universities, are *ronin*.

Most *yobiko* are situated in big cities, where the majority of universities are also located. There is fierce competition between the schools, each of which claims to be the best and the most effective at getting students into the top universities. Tuition is expensive: at the Keioshingakukai school, Saitama Prefecture, for example, in the 1998 school year, regular full-time attendees paid ¥590,000 ($4,720) for annual tuition without room and board and ¥2,000,000 ($16,000) with room and board.

Ronin who fail entrance exams a second time may try yet again. Those who are determined to enter a prestigious university continue to study at *yobiko* for as long as necessary. Some students fail the exams three times or more in a row, but they do not give up, because their parents are willing to provide financial aid, and because a degree from a top university is a kind of passport to a successful career.

Chapter 6: Higher Education

The college entrance ratio has been rising. In 1950, a little over 10 % of high school graduates (15 % of males and 5 % of females) entered higher education. The figure rose to about 25 % in 1970 and to almost 38 % in 1975. By 1997, almost half (47.3 %) of high school graduates went on to higher education.

Japanese universities are said to be a "leisure land" where students enjoy hobbies and social activities before graduating with ease. In contrast with the laborious work of the high school years, college years are, generally speaking, a time of relaxed study and play. Unlike the schools, the universities do not have classes on Saturdays. Besides, students are not pressurized into attending classes, and often faculty do not show up either. Exams and written assignments are few; expectations for performance on tests are low. Lenient assessment is widespread, allowing students to pass without much study and to obtain credits without regular class attendance.

In the final year, students look for post-graduation jobs. Most large corporations base recruitment simply on the prestige of the candidate's university rather than on what each individual may have learned. The assumption must be that to have entered that university at all the student must have studied diligently at high school and so will make a hard-working employee.

Types of Higher Educational Institution

There are three types of higher educational institutions: university, junior college and vocational college. The universities are centers of advanced knowledge and in-depth research in specialized academic disciplines. Most first degree courses last four years (six years for medical, dental and veterinary courses). A master's degree usually requires two years of study, a doctorate five years (four years for medical, dental or veterinary courses). The junior college offers practical lessons and specialized research. As with universities, applicants must have completed high school or its equivalent, but courses are shorter, lasting two or three years. Successful junior college students are awarded the title of associate. The vocational college provides practical and technical training. To enable each vocational college to have its own distinct curriculum and meet the diverse learning needs of students, the national standard regulations for vocational schools are more flexible than for the other institutions. Most vocational colleges offer one or two year training courses, whose standard is roughly equivalent to that of junior colleges. Nursing and English courses are popular for women, and car maintenance or computer science courses for men.

About 80 % of universities and junior colleges are co-educational; the rest are women's universities and junior colleges - there are no men's universities and junior colleges. A majority of university students are males since female students tend to favor two-year college courses rather than four years at university. English, psychology and nursing are the most popular courses among female students.

Modern telecommunications have enabled the government to establish the University of the Air. Founded in 1983, this offers thousands of people lifelong learning opportunities using television, radio and other diverse media. In fiscal 1997, its education via satellite became available nationwide. As of March 1996, there were 8,340 graduates of the University of the Air.

Funding

While the operating expenses of public institutions of higher education are funded by the national or local governments, private institutions must rely heavily on tuition and other student fees. However, to promote teaching and research activities of private institutions, which outnumber the public, and to reduce the financial burden of enrolled students, the Education Ministry offers financial aid and favorable tax measures. In fiscal 1970, the ministry started to subsidize private higher education. In fiscal 1997, private universities were provided with ¥370 billion ($2.96 billion), accounting for about 10 % of their total operating expenses.

The Academic Year

The academic year runs from April to March, and is not split into terms. Teaching takes place from mid-April to mid-July, from October to mid-December, and in early January. The final week of September is reserved for mid-term exams, and final exams take place at the end of January. Some classes also hold seminars in summer.

In most universities, the freshman and sophomore years are spent primarily on general subjects, while in the last two years students focus on their area of specialization. This is in contrast to junior and vocational colleges, where students take both general and specialized subjects from the beginning. Students are not allowed to change their majors once they have been admitted to school, because the entrant selection is done on a departmental basis. If students wish to transfer to another university they must take the appropriate entrance exam, so transfers and withdrawals are rare.

Foreign Students

After a sharp rise in the numbers of overseas students in Japan between the mid-1980s and the mid-1990s, the trend is now in decline.   As of May 1, 1997 there were 51,047 overseas students, down 1,874 from the previous year. Foreign students account for only about 1.5 % of the total student body, compared with 10 % overseas students in Britain and 7 % in France. Recognizing the value to learning and to international relations of having a large international student body, the Education Ministry has tried to reverse the decline, bringing in a range of measures including improvement of the Japanese government's scholarship program; promotion of short-term study programs; financial aid to those studying at their own expense; assistance with living accommodation; improvements to teaching and guidance; improved access to information on study in Japan, and follow-up services after the students' return home.   So far, however, these measures have been unsuccessful.

There are a number of reasons for the decline of the number of foreign students. Japan's current economic turmoil means that living costs are far higher than in other industrialized countries; there is insufficient information abroad about higher education and government grants in Japan; and Japan's school officials tend not to understand the importance of global exchange of personnel. Moreover, Japan's rigid university admission system, with only one enrollment per year, presents problems for foreign students who seek summer or fall enrollment. The Japanese Proficiency Test (JPT), which foreign students are required to pass, is also held only once a year: if applicants cannot take the test on that day they must wait a year for another chance. Japanese students wishing to attend universities in English-speaking countries face no such problems: the TOEFL (Test of English as a Foreign Language) is given every month.

However, perhaps the most important reason for the relatively small number of foreign students studying in Japan is the closed nature of Japanese society. Foreigners, especially westerners, are assumed to be unable to speak Japanese and are regarded as alien. Since most Japanese people have poor command of English, they are afraid of contact with the "aliens." In an overcrowded bus or train, for example, Japanese passengers do not sit next to western-looking people, and bus drivers or conductors ignore them or do not provide them with necessary information. Foreign students who have problems living in Japan cannot expect much help from Japanese people.

Those overseas students who do make it to Japanese universities are permitted to work a maximum 28 hours a week during school terms to help support their studies. During extended school holidays, they are allowed to work up to eight hours a day. Before they take up employment, they must gain permission from the Justice Ministry.

Japanese Students Abroad

The Education Ministry encourages students to study abroad and provides qualified students with scholarship programs. According to a UNESCO (United Nations Educational, Scientific and Cultural Organization) survey, in 1996 about 60,000 Japanese went abroad in pursuit of higher education, twice as many as five years before. The most popular destination was the United States.

Japanese students in the United States do not make many American friends, but tend instead to group together, even after the initial culture shock has been overcome. Such group dependence may be explained, at least in part, by religious differences between the two countries. In the United States, many people follow the Christian faith, which holds that all are equal before God. In Japan,

207

the rich are praised and the poor are condemned. It is extremely difficult for Japanese expatriates, accustomed to the pecking order of Japanese society, to absorb or recognize the American way of liberal thinking.

The Rank Order of the Universities

Like high schools, universities are arranged in a hierarchy, based on reputation. Tokyo University is the most prestigious, followed by Kyoto University, Waseda University and Keio University. (Tokyo and Kyoto are national institutions; Waseda and Keio are private.) The top universities accept only the brightest, most academically able, students. Indeed, since university admission depends almost exclusively on entrance exam scores, it is possible to work out a student's scholastic level simply by knowing which university he or she attends.

The rank-order system means that high-performing students look down on below-average students. In this extract from the *Yomiuri* "Troubleshooter" column (July 4, 1998), a senior student at a national university tells how she judges other people by their scholastic ability:

Don't forget all the people who got you to the top

Dear Troubleshooter: I am a fourth-year student at a national university. I entered the university directly from high school and my grades are always the highest among my peers. Probably because I think that I am the best, I sometimes abuse my mother and younger brother, who I think are inferior to me, as far as superficial things like education go. Once when my mother spilled a little sauce on the table, I said disagreeable things to her. When my brother, who started to work at a small factory this spring, consulted me about something, I let him down, saying that he should have known how to handle such a simple matter as he was already 18 years old. I am about to take an examination to become a civil servant. If I fail this, it will be my first failure in life. So I feel irritated these days. But whenever I relax, I regret what I have said to my mother and brother. When I think about how I judge people this way, I worry that I am becoming a narrow-mined person. Please give some advice. Miss R

Dear Miss R: You are wonderful. You are fighting with yourself because you place a high priority on grades and your academic career, yet you worry about not being kind enough to your mother and brother. You are right. There is no direct connection between having excellent grades at school and being an excellent human being. Your grades are the result of a combination of talent - which you inherited from your parents - the environment you grew up in, getting enough love from your parents, being in good enough health to endure the hardship of study, good teachers and friends, and your own efforts. You did not get to the top alone. Thank the people around you and be modest. Even if you pass the coming examination, you will still experience many failures in your job and future human relationships. However, failures help you grow. If you continue to reflect on yourself by reading many books, encouraging many people and experiencing many things, I am sure you will become a charming woman. Osaka University professor

Miss R, however, is an exception. Most elite students do not regret their attitudes towards others, but are convinced that their decisions and behavior are justified, and that their excellent test scores mark them out as virtuous and responsible. At the same time, people with lesser school achievements feel inferior and are frustrated.

Education Expenditures and Scholarship

Education and living expenses for university students are rising constantly. In the 1996 academic year, tuition and living expenses for undergraduate students averaged ¥1,941,000 ($15,500), up almost ¥100,000 ($800), or about 5 % from two years earlier, according to a biennial survey by the Education Ministry. The average annual expenditure per undergraduate comprised ¥1,065,000 ($8,500) in tuition fees and ¥876,000 ($7,000) in living expenses. Private university students living apart from their families spent an average of ¥2,542,000 ($20,300) annually. In the 1998 academic year the entrance fee for national universities was ¥275,000 ($2,200) and annual tuition fees were about ¥470,000 ($3,760). The average annual tuition fees of private universities, including an entrance fee, were about ¥1,060,000 ($8,480).

Students rely heavily on their parents to pay for tuition and living expenses. The biennial survey found that students were given an average of ¥1,562,000 ($12,500) in allowances, up ¥147,000 ($1,176), or 10.4 % from the previous survey and accounting for three-fourths of their average total incomes of ¥2,066,000 ($16,500). Most parents can afford this. The survey found that the average annual income per household of students at national universities was ¥9,719,000 ($77,700), a 7.3 % rise. For parents of private university students, the average income was ¥10,075,000 ($80,600), surpassing ¥10,000,000 ($80,000) for the first time. These figures indicate a strong connection between family income and university attendance.

Students who lack adequate funds to pay for tuition fees can apply for financial aid programs run by the Japan Scholarship Foundation, which is financed by the national government. Scholarship loans bearing either no interest or low interest are granted to competent students who cannot afford to attend higher educational institutions. In 1996, the Foundation provided approximately ¥239.3 billion ($1.9 billion) to about 484,000 students. Other financial aid programs are run by local governments, non-profit corporations or individual educational institutions.

The Wide Disparity between High School and University Education

According to a survey conducted by a study group at the request of the Education Ministry, more than two-thirds of freshmen are concerned about their ability to understand college lectures. The problem seems particularly acute among students taking science courses, where 85.1 % of respondents cited problems based on their own lack of knowledge or enthusiasm, and the poor quality of lectures. Students also felt that high school had not concentrated enough on writing skills or foreign languages.

Analyzing the results of the survey, the study group concluded that there was a wide disparity between high school and university education: high schools focus on simple rote learning, while universities nurture analytical skills. The study group reported to the Central Council for Education, recommending that students take many different subjects at high school in order to prepare for study at the university level.

The Academic Curriculum and Studies

To graduate university students are required to earn, on average, 120 credits in four years. A standard class of 90 minutes once a week for 30 weeks counts as three credits. Most students take 10 unit hours (10 classes) a week so that the total number of credits is 30 a year. While the average class size is 40, classes of over 100 are common in the humanities and social sciences.

Most students study little in the freshman and sophomore years. On most courses there are few quizzes, chapter tests, mid-term exams or written assignments, and attendance registers are rarely taken. Some students earn credits without attending classes at all; they use lecture notes borrowed from their peers to prepare for the final exams which determine who passes and fails. However, foreign language classes are more demanding. The roll is always called and reading or translation assignments are given at each class. In a typical English class, a student will read two pages of a textbook aloud and translate a paragraph into Japanese.

In the junior and senior years, engineering and natural science majors need to work very hard. They follow a highly structured curriculum, spending hours each day on experiments and training in the lab offices, and writing a senior thesis in their fourth year. A typical lab office consists of a professor, an assistant professor, several graduate students, and several juniors and seniors. Students develop close relationships with their professors and each other through studies and research, remaining in the same lab office with the same professor until graduation. Graduate students, who are not allowed to become teaching assistants in Japan, help undergraduate students without being paid. In some ways, these lab offices recall middle and high schools: the close personal ties, similar to the peer group socialization of extracurricular club activities, exist alongside a rigid hierarchy of professors, graduate students and undergraduate students, similar to the pecking order of teachers, upperclassmen and lower-grade students.

Compared with engineering and natural science students, humanities and social science students have a less stressful life in the junior and senior years. They are required to attend a seminar once a week for two consecutive years with the same professor. The seminar - the equivalent of a lab office - comprises a professor and 15-20 students who engage in debate and research. In addition to topics selected by the professor, students can choose their own discussion themes. Each student gives a presentation, followed by questions. Although many seminar classes require seniors to write a thesis based on their research, there are no substantial research assignments in the third year. Taking advantage of this, most humanities students gain enough credits to graduate in three years, and only attend seminars in the fourth year while doing part-time work, club activities and job-hunting.

Faculty Staff and Nepotism

University instructors must have a Ph.D. or an MA, as well as university teaching and research experience and a publication record. Exceptions are made only for native speaker language teachers, who may be employed without an MA or any publications. However, whilst these basic requirements are known, recruitment methods are not open: there is neither faculty-wide selection organization nor clarification of decision-making methods nor active dissemination of employment information. In fact, faculty members are often employed on the basis of personal connection or nepotism, which is nurtured by group socialization in lab offices or seminars in each department. Thus, each university selects staff from among its own graduates, while "outsiders" with diverse backgrounds and experience, including graduates of other universities, are not employed.

University nepotism leads to stagnant teaching and lenient evaluations of students. Faculty members are guaranteed life-long employment, regardless of their teaching skills and research performance, and thus they tend to become negligent in their duties. They do not hold "office hours," and give the same lectures and exams year after year, using the same textbooks. Classes are usually one-way lectures, with no class discussion. Some

215

instructors even forbid questions during class, regarding these as a challenge to their authority. Moreover, since instructors have discretion to decide course requirements and the strictness of grading, these are pitched very low, making the instructors' lives easier. In consequence, students are neither motivated nor inspired to study, and many decide to skip classes.

It will not be easy to find a way to change the complacency and cronyism within universities. Most universities currently have a self-assessment panel to monitor university education, research and management, but this system does not function properly, precisely because of cronyism - panel staff are unable fairly to evaluate their fellow faculty members. To revitalize higher education in Japan, universities will need to introduce a checking system such as an independent assessment committee administered by external experts, who objectively monitor professors' teaching skills and research performance. Only experts brought in from outside can effectively keep university nepotism in check.

Part-time Work and Leisure Activities

Students take part-time work in various industries: post offices, fast-food restaurants, supermarkets, convenience stores, swimming pools, etc. Indeed the service industries rely on student workers. The most popular and comparatively well paid job, however, is as private tutor or *juku* teacher of English, math and other subjects to primary, middle, or high school students. The pay varies about from ¥2,000 ($16) to ¥4,000 ($32) per hour, depending on the level of the lessons and the status of their university - Tokyo students are paid most. In 1997 the average annual income from part-time work of high school, college and university students in the Tokyo area was ¥509,000 ($4,072), up ¥42,000 ($336) from the previous year. The average hourly wage was ¥1,017, and students worked, on average, 106.4 days a year. As their parents usually pay their living expenses and any tuition fees, most students use their earnings for leisure activities, such as bowling, skiing, camping and hiking; playing tennis and golf; or traveling abroad during the summer or winter vacation.

Club Activities

Large universities have hundreds of academic, sports, arts or hobby-oriented clubs. Some sports clubs (athletic sports, football, baseball, basketball, karate, etc) train their members hard in order to win national competitions, but most are purely recreational organizations. Many male students join a club with the sole aim of finding a girlfriend. Indeed clubs actively recruit female members in April, the beginning of the academic year, in the campus or from women's universities. Club activities usually begin at 4 p.m. after classes and last about two hours. Then many members go to eat and drink beer or sake (rice wine) together, and perhaps sing at a karaoke bar. This costs about ¥3,000 ($24) per person, including food and drinks. Clubs also organize skiing trips in winter, hiking in the spring and fall, and swimming in the summer. Such a heavy entertainment schedule leaves little time for study.

The clubs are very hierarchic, especially for the males, just like the extracurricular clubs at middle and high schools. First-year members are expected to pay respect to older students by bowing every time they meet and by obeying orders, for example to buy a pack of cigarettes from a nearby store. Senior students are thus "kings," freshmen "slaves." The hierarchy is established at a welcome party for new members in April when male students are forced to drink large quantities of beer and sake as an initiation. Some quit the club, but many new members remain, continuing to tolerate subservience until they, in turn, become upperclassmen and discipline new comers next year. They are also dissuaded from leaving by the fact that senior students traditionally pay the largest share of eating and drinking expenses, perhaps ¥20,000 ($160) of a ¥25,000 ($200) bar check, allowing newcomers to wine and dine very cheaply. In other words, elder students take care of first-year students financially in exchange for their obedience.

Volunteer Activities

According to a 1997 survey by the Center for Domestic and Foreign Students, 80 % of college students put part-time employment before volunteer activities. While 95% of respondents had held a part-time job at some time, only 41 % (50 % of the females and 35 % of the males) had participated in a volunteer activity. Only 7 % were doing any voluntary activity at the time of the survey. Most who volunteered were education or social-welfare major students. 47% of volunteer participants instructed sports to children, and 36 % took care of elderly or disabled people.

The top three reasons for not doing more voluntary work were a busy college life (53 %), lack of knowledge or skill (46 %), and insufficient information on such activities (43 %) (multiple responses permitted). However, the survey attributes the unpopularity of voluntary activity partly to the general emphasis on money in the affluent Japanese society. Fifty percent of respondents said that reward was necessary, while only 18% said that payment was unimportant. An education professor said that some payment for voluntary activities would increase the number of student participants.

Employment

In the late 1980s about 80% of graduates found immediate employment. Economic recession has reduced this figure considerably and increased the competition among students for jobs. According to a survey released in July, 1998 of 1,243 institutions nationwide, students at universities, junior colleges and professional schools started searching for work about a month earlier than in the previous year, consequently classroom attendance was down. To minimize disruption of studies universities have asked the Japan Federation of Employers Associations to ensure companies' recruiting activities are held on holidays.

According to the Education Ministry, the number of college graduates in 1998 was a record high of about 529,000. However, only 65.6% (66.2 % males, 64.5 % females) had found full-time employment by May 1, 1998 - the lowest proportion since 1951 and 2,000 fewer than in 1997. About 50,000 or 9.4 % were entering graduate schools or other institutions for further education; about

12,000 or 2.2 % had taken part-time or temporary jobs; about 82,000 or 15.5 %, a record high, were unemployed.

Students take their job-hunting very seriously. They are eager to be employed by large, famous companies in pursuit of a high salary, good prospects for promotion and stability of management. It is believed that the larger the company is, the more its workers have financial security and the less the possibility of bankruptcy. Workers are expected to stay with the same firm for years, preferably until retirement, and companies prepare their employee education and training programs, and develop their salary and promotion systems, with this in mind. Large corporations incorporate superior employee training and pay hike systems into their life-long employment policy, so whoever is hired by top companies will enjoy life-long economic stability.

The most important reason for applying to a large corporation is, however, the "rank order" of the companies. As with universities, there is a hierarchy of companies in Japan, and people are judged by the company to which they belong, not by their profession. Employees in famous corporations are thought of as superior to those hired by small companies in terms of intelligence and personal prestige, to say nothing of earnings. Students who are offered employment in famous companies gain fame for themselves and honor for their families, just as they did by passing the entrance exams of top universities.

Students' zeal to find employment with large companies means that they start looking for a job by collecting employment information as early as the senior year, and begin job-hunting in earnest after the final exam in the third year. Many students visit several companies and meet firms' personnel representatives, even before completing enrollment procedures for the next academic year. The time and effort put into job-hunting means that students cannot afford to attend classes on a regular basis. To ensure that they have enough credits for graduation, a majority of students obtain enough credits to graduate in three years and take only one or two classes in the fourth year. Furthermore, some universities ease graduation requirements to accommodate those who cut classes for job-hunting. Students attending employment seminars or taking recruitment examinations are given credit without going to classes. They are often allowed six officially permitted absences a year per subject.

While students apply to large corporations, companies look for promising graduates, particularly those from prestigious universities. Qualified candidates are screened through individual and group interviews, in which each applicant's character and personality is examined and assessed against the needs of the company. Particular emphasis is placed on leadership qualities, so leaders of clubs (especially sports clubs) are highly favored. Recruiters may take into consideration an applicant's scholastic ability and knowledge, but a student's major is not a main selection criterion, because companies expect new employees to undergo on-the-job training.

As with universities, nepotism is widespread in recruitment to large corporations, especially with regard to students majoring in engineering and science. Corporate recruiters develop and maintain good relationships with engineering and science professors by sponsoring projects in lab offices or in the universities, and they hire a fixed number of graduates each year, even in times of recession. The professors, for their part, provide the companies with promising students. Even here though, those who belong to lab offices of famous universities are at an advantage.

Large corporations are said to have completed their selection of candidates in mid-May for employment the following April. Students who fail to gain offers of employment from large companies continue to hunt for jobs in medium and small-sized businesses. In general, students of top universities go to top companies, while students of other universities are hired by medium and small-sized businesses. This practice is inevitable, due to the "rank orders" of companies and universities, leading to the further increase in the disparity between members of the elite and the non-elite.

On April 1, each company holds an entrance ceremony and an orientation for its new graduate employees, who listen solemnly to a speech by the company president, as school children attend to the principal. Workers are very obedient to their bosses, as younger students are subject to upperclassmen in club activities at schools. Male employees in particular are loyal to their companies, give the highest priority to their jobs, and work long and hard, even sacrificing their personal lives. Indeed, the "separation of work and personal life," normal in American society, is alien to Japan. Japanese workers belong to their companies rather than to themselves, placing group interests above individual freedom.

Although many companies do not hire, train or promote female graduates, regarding women as auxiliaries in a male-dominated corporate structure, most Japanese women are too passive - unlike their American counterparts - to demonstrate against companies. Instead, they call on the government to enact a law to abolish sexism in the workplace. However laws, a set of citizens' "minimum" obligations, will not be enough to change the discriminatory corporate structure. Female workers are still expected to quit as soon as they get married or have children. They are generally denied maternity leave or child-care leave. Moreover, female workers remain very vulnerable to sexual harassment by their male bosses.

Corporate Views on University Education

The University Council, an advisory panel to the Education Minister, deliberates on measures to raise the level of instruction and facilitate better management. Most companies and students, however, are content to regard university as a fun-oriented break between the long and hard study of high school and the diligent commitment of employment. Companies do not expect university education to be relevant or practical. As knowledge from lectures is usually useless in business, the companies develop their own training programs for new employees. Meanwhile, the current university system enables students to enjoy themselves for a while.

Reforms to the University System: the University Council's 1994 Reports

1) Report on Improvement of Employment Procedures

The University Council's report, "Improvement of Teaching Staff Employment Procedures," (June 1994) made the following recommendations:

- Universities should actively employ people with diverse backgrounds and experience, including people graduated from or with experience in other universities, as well as non-academics and women.
- Universities should make greater use of the system of open recruitment.
- When determining selection criteria for teaching staff, it is necessary to take into account the philosophies and objectives of individual universities and faculties. In future it will also be increasingly important to evaluate educational abilities actively and to appraise research abilities with the emphasis on quality.
- Steps should be taken to ensure that the methods used to select teaching staff are open, including the formation of faculty-wide or university-wide selection organizations consisting of teaching staff in related fields and efforts to obtain outside appraisals and recommendations.
- Efforts should be made to improve the quality of teaching staff at both the graduate-student and faculty levels. In particular, organized efforts are needed to improve educational content and teaching methods.
- Teaching staff from abroad should be employed more actively.

2) Report on Management

The report entitled "Facilitation of University Management" made the following recommendations:

- University presidents should exercise greater leadership in promoting university reform and coping positively with social change. Innovation is needed in such areas as the selection and terms of office of university presidents, the level of assistance provided, and budgetary allocations in order to facilitate the exercise of leadership by university presidents.

- National universities and local public universities need to develop new ways of managing their senates. It is also necessary to select agenda items for deliberation with care and to clarify and simplify procedures. Private universities should develop organizations to coordinate university-wide teaching and to centralize and integrate decisions.
- It is necessary to modify faculty dean appointment methods and terms of office and establish support systems according to the circumstances in individual faculties to enable faculty deans to exercise greater leadership.
- Faculty meetings need to select agenda items for deliberation with care and to establish systems appropriate to those items. It is also necessary to modify decision-making methods, including clarification of the decision-making process, through the introduction of voting or other methods.
- Administrative organizations need to be constantly reviewed and improved.
- Priorities from the perspective of open management include the active dissemination of university information, local and global contributions, and efforts to reflect the views of students in university management.
- Coordination and communication between school corporation management, such as boards of regents, and educational organizations are vital.

The Education Ministry also revised the "National Standards for the Establishment of Universities," to allow universities more freedom in organizing a curriculum and making respective changes.

The University Council's 1998 Interim Report

On June 30, 1998, the University Council released an interim report on the ideal role of universities and how to meet the needs of higher education in the 21st century. It called for large-scale reforms to the current university system, including stricter assessment of students' academic performance, provision for the early graduation of exceptional students, and the expansion of graduate schools. Stricter evaluations may lead to an increased number of repeat students, and the report requests that the Education Ministry take necessary measures to deal with this.

High rates of absenteeism among students are attributed in part to the one-way lecture system, which brings about little teacher-student interaction in the classroom. Instructors are suggested to make students earn their grades through constant class performance, in addition to test results and class attendance.

The report indicates that it is lenient evaluations that enable students to obtain enough credits to graduate in three years and devote their fourth year to job-hunting. Universities are advised to limit the number of credits that students can take in a term or a year so that they study more per credit.

First-year students currently have difficulty in understanding some subjects, because they did not study them at high school. To smooth the transition from high school to university, the report recommends that universities set up supplementary courses or suggest subjects to be introduced into high schools, so that students are better prepared for study at the university level.

The current university system requires that students complete undergraduate degrees after four years. To make university education more flexible, the report proposes that universities allow students with high grades to graduate in three years, and permit senior students to graduate in the fall, six months earlier than the end of the regular academic year, to enable them to enroll at graduate schools abroad.

The report suggests that national universities expand the role of graduate schools by reducing the number of undergraduate courses. Graduate schools, which currently instruct students to become researchers, are expected to focus more on vocational education, on the lines of U.S. business schools and law schools, with the aim of training the country's business managers and legal experts. Short-term graduate courses such as one-year business administration courses, as well as part-time study programs are also suggested to assist businesspeople and encourage the enrollment of mature students.

More than half of the proposals made in the interim report are supported by university presidents, according to a Kyodo News survey released on October 25, 1998. The survey polled 65 public universities and 41 private universities, of which 57 public and 38 private universities responded. Fifty-eight universities, or about 60 % of the total, were in favor of granting permission to students with high marks to graduate in three years instead of the current four, although most universities said that for the new system to be implemented, it would be necessary to evaluate students more strictly. Forty universities said that they were capable of introducing a strict grading system, while 34 said that strict evaluations were possible only in classes with a small number of students. Nine private universities said that they held a number of classes in huge lecture theaters with little teacher-student interaction, so that they were unable to strictly grade students on their individual performance. Sixty-seven universities, or about 70 % of the total, said that they wanted to introduce a one-year master's degree program or study its feasibility in order to attract working people to graduate school, while 18 responded in the negative.

The University Council's 1998 Final Report

The University Council's final report, submitted on October 26, 1998, argues that Japan's universities are closed institutions, not accountable to the public. The self-assessment system to improve teaching, research and management, used by 90% of Japan's universities, is a mere formality, unable to drive through reforms. To prevent stagnation, corruption and irresponsibility, the report strongly urges the establishment of an independent panel of external experts, operating on principals of transparency, to assess universities' standards of education, research and management. The Education Ministry would in part determine budgetary allocations by reference to the assessments, giving more funding to those with highest marks. The report also advocates that each university set up its own advisory council of independent experts, with a chairperson approved by the Education Minister, to monitor and advise on administration and management when requested by the university president.

The report suggests that the unclear division of responsibilities between university presidents, councils and faculties prevents quick, effective decision-making. It urges university boards of trustees, which comprise the university president and faculty deans, to limit the role of faculty councils so that the presidents can exercise greater leadership, with the help of an advisory board of vice presidents and presidential appointees. It is the presidents' duty to clarify administrators' responsibilities and to promote the revision of academic curricula and the enhancement of research. Such strong leadership would enable each university to have its own distinctive color. To balance this increased power, however, the presidents must disclose information and operate open management.

Some education analysts have criticized the proposals as insufficient, claiming that universities will remain stagnant while the Education Ministry controls each university's budgetary allocation and appoints university administrators. To give universities more autonomy, the critics call for the transformation of the legal status of national universities to that of independent administrative corporations. The Education Ministry strongly opposes this, determined to keep total control over state-run universities. The report reserves judgment, saying that the issue needs long-term discussion. The University Council seems reluctant to make reform proposals incompatible with the traditional views of the ministry.

On March 9, 1999 the ministry submitted the bills, based on the interim and final reports, to the Diet for the revision of the School Education Law and four other related laws. It plans to begin implementing most of the changes to state-run universities in spring 2000.

Appendix

The Number of Schools, Teachers and Students, based on surveys by the Education Ministry

The Number of Schools

	National	Public	Private
Kindergartens in Fiscal 1996	49	6,140	8,601
Elementary Schools in Fiscal 1996	73	24,235	174
Middle Schools in Fiscal 1996	78	10,537	654
High Schools in Fiscal 1996	17	4,164	1,315
Technical Colleges in Fiscal 1995	54	5	3
Vocational Schools in Fiscal 1996	148	223	3,141
Miscellaneous Schools in Fiscal 1996	3	55	2,656
Junior Colleges in Fiscal 1995	36	60	500
Universities in Fiscal 1995	98	52	415

The Number of Teachers in Schools

	Males	Females
Kindergartens in Fiscal 1996	6,235	97,283
Elementary Schools in Fiscal 1996	163,477	262,237
Middle Schools in Fiscal 1996	163,204	207,768
High Schools in Fiscal 1996	212,404	66,475
Technical College in Fiscal 1995	4,178	128
Vocational Schools in Fiscal 1996	18,657	18,173
Miscellaneous Schools in Fiscal 1996	9,795	5,997
Junior College in Fiscal 1995	12,469	8,233
Universities in Fiscal 1995	122,712	14,752

The Number of Students Enrolled in Schools

	Males	Females
Kindergartens in Fiscal 1996	912,111	885,940
Elementary Schools in Fiscal 1996	4,148,218	3,957,411
Middle Schools in Fiscal 1996	2,314,237	2,213,163
High Schools in Fiscal 1996	2,284,283	2,263,214
Technical Colleges in Fiscal 1995	46,268	9,966
Vocational Schools in Fiscal 1996	384,352	415,199
Miscellaneous Schools in Fiscal 1996	153,738	152,806
Junior Colleges in Fiscal 1995	43,077	455,439
Universities in Fiscal 1995	1,724,756	821,893
Graduate Students with Master's Degrees in Fiscal 1996	85,269	24,380
Graduate Students with Doctorate Degrees in Fiscal 1996	35,164	8,610

Printed in the United States
205667BV00001B/44/A

9 781581 127997